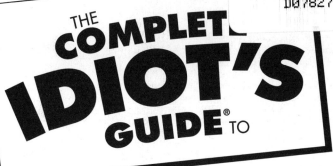

THE **COMPLETE IDIOT'S GUIDE®** TO

Enhancing Sexual Desire

by Judy Ford, MSW, LCSW and
Rachel Greene Baldino, MSW, LCSW

ALPHA

A member of Penguin Group (USA) Inc.

ALPHA BOOKS

Published by the Penguin Group
Penguin Group (USA) Inc., 375 Hudson Street, New York, New York 10014, USA
Penguin Group (Canada), 90 Eglinton Avenue East, Suite 700, Toronto, Ontario M4P 2Y3, Canada (a division of Pearson Penguin Canada Inc.)
Penguin Books Ltd., 80 Strand, London WC2R 0RL, England
Penguin Ireland, 25 St. Stephen's Green, Dublin 2, Ireland (a division of Penguin Books Ltd.)
Penguin Group (Australia), 250 Camberwell Road, Camberwell, Victoria 3124, Australia (a division of Pearson Australia Group Pty. Ltd.)
Penguin Books India Pvt. Ltd., 11 Community Centre, Panchsheel Park, New Delhi—110 017, India
Penguin Group (NZ), 67 Apollo Drive, Rosedale, North Shore, Auckland 1311, New Zealand (a division of Pearson New Zealand Ltd.)
Penguin Books (South Africa) (Pty.) Ltd., 24 Sturdee Avenue, Rosebank, Johannesburg 2196, South Africa
Penguin Books Ltd., Registered Offices: 80 Strand, London WC2R 0RL, England

Copyright © 2007 by Judy Ford and Rachel Greene Baldino

International Standard Book Number: 978-1-59257-678-4
Library of Congress Catalog Card Number: 2007930854

09 08 07   8 7 6 5 4 3 2 1

Interpretation of the printing code: The rightmost number of the first series of numbers is the year of the book's printing; the rightmost number of the second series of numbers is the number of the book's printing. For example, a printing code of 07-1 shows that the first printing occurred in 2007.

Printed in the United States of America

Note: This publication contains the opinions and ideas of its authors. It is intended to provide helpful and informative material on the subject matter covered. It is sold with the understanding that the authors and publisher are not engaged in rendering professional services in the book. If the reader requires personal assistance or advice, a competent professional should be consulted.

The authors and publisher specifically disclaim any responsibility for any liability, loss, or risk, personal or otherwise, which is incurred as a consequence, directly or indirectly, of the use and application of any of the contents of this book.

Most Alpha books are available at special quantity discounts for bulk purchases for sales promotions, premiums, fund-raising, or educational use. Special books, or book excerpts, can also be created to fit specific needs.

For details, write: Special Markets, Alpha Books, 375 Hudson Street, New York, NY 10014.

Publisher: *Marie Butler-Knight*
Editorial Director: *Mike Sanders*
Managing Editor: *Billy Fields*
Acquisitions Editor: *Paul Dinas*
Development Editor: *Susan Zingraf*
Production Editor: *Megan Douglass*
Copy Editor: *Jan Zoya*

Cartoonist: *Shannon Wheeler*
Cover Designer: *Bill Thomas*
Book Designer: *Trina Wurst*
Indexer: *Heather McNeill*
Layout: *Chad Dressler*
Proofreader: *Mary Hunt*

To the many couples who have shared with me the creative ways that they keep their love alive. Judy Ford

For my husband Michael. Rachel Greene Baldino

Contents at a Glance

Appendixes

Contents

Appendixes

Introduction

You can feel passionate again. Sexy again. You can get the urge again. Reading this book is the beginning of that exciting, sensuous adventure. It will broaden your relationship and help you reach new heights of pleasure. If you read the book and do the exercises, you will discover a new dimension of intimacy. The more familiar you are with all the ingredients that go into making a passionate liaison, the better lover you will become and the happier your connection will be.

Your relationship is precious; you love your partner and you have enjoyed expressing your love through joyful sexual intimacy. But lately you've been discouraged. The desire you once felt has faded. You'd like to feel the physical spark again, but you're not sure how to revive it or where to begin. Perhaps you're confused and wonder if the sexual pleasure you once shared is gone forever. Perhaps you feel alone in your struggle, not knowing what steps to take. If you have ever felt this way, then let us reassure you that you have come to the right place. This book can help.

You are not alone in this dilemma. Most couples go through dry spells, periods of inhibited desire, and lack of emotional and sexual intimacy. There are times when all couples feel distant and not as close as they once did. The good news is that this does not have to remain a permanent condition. Couples who are willing to investigate the source of diminished desire, willing to learn new behaviors, and to communicate openly do experience a return to passion. In other words, if you are willing to read this book and do the work, you can revitalize your union. There is hope for the two of you!

As you begin reading, you will realize that low desire does not have to be a tragedy. On the contrary, low desire, while troublesome, is a common occurrence in most modern relationships.

How This Book Is Organized

This book is divided into three parts covering the basis, need and skills for enhancing sexual desire.

In **Part 1, Let's Talk About Sex,** we discuss the importance of making love with your partner. Your sexual relationship is part of the emotional glue that bonds you and keeps you close, even when you are going through a rough patch ... and nearly all couples experience rough patches at one point or another. In this part, you'll learn all about the stages of love relationships, the importance of "generous gestures," how strong communication can enhance a couple's sex life, and the many roles of sex in a couple's relationship.

Part 2, Getting in Touch with Your Sensuality, delves into sexual desire and arousal as deeply personal experiences; what drives one person wild with passion may do absolutely nothing for another (and vice versa). Also, how you feel about yourself translates into how you feel, act, and respond in the bedroom. This part will familiarize you with the physical and emotional dimensions of sexual desire and arousal, and help you figure out what makes you and your partner feel sexy, turned on, and connected.

In **Part 3, Prioritizing Your Relationship,** we look at children, careers, and life's never-ending and ever-changing list of responsibilities that often leave little time or energy for your relationship with your partner. The chapters in this part focus on understanding the different areas of your life that need and require your time and attention—your couple relationship, your family, and your work—and how to achieve a healthy balance between them all. You'll find creative, practical tips and strategies for making your relationship with your partner one of your absolute top priorities and your sexual desire soar to new heights.

Insights for the Reader

Throughout the book, you'll find these notes with helpful information and interesting tidbits to help you learn more about sexual desire and how to enhance it.

def•i•ni•tion
Terms and explanations relating to sex drive and desire.

Love Booster
Helpful bits of advice designed to turn up the heat in the bedroom.

Mood Killer _____

Activities or behaviors to steer clear of to help get your sex life back on track.

Notable Quotable _____

Quotes from experts and clients on what really works to keep passion alive in a relationship.

Acknowledgments

None of these words would have been delivered to the page without Rachel Baldino, my co-author, Andrea Hurst, literary agent, and Paul Dinas, editor. Thank you all for including me and making our working relationship go smoothly.—Judy Ford

I would like to thank Judy Ford for her wisdom, insight, and collaborative spirit. I am also grateful to Paul Dinas, Susan Zingraf, Megan Douglass, and Jan Zoya for their detailed and attentive editorial guidance. And I am deeply indebted to my agent, Andrea Hurst, for bringing all of us together. On a more personal note, for their unflagging love and encouragement, I thank my husband Michael, my children Justin and Emily, my parents Robert and Judith, my brother and sister-in-law Sean and Sarah, my parents-in-law, Phyllis and Louis, and all of my supportive family members and friends.—Rachel Greene Baldino

Trademarks

All terms mentioned in this book that are known to be or are suspected of being trademarks or service marks have been appropriately capitalized. Alpha Books and Penguin Group (USA) Inc. cannot attest to the accuracy of this information. Use of a term in this book should not be regarded as affecting the validity of any trademark or service mark.

Part 1

Let's Talk About Sex

Making love with your partner is important for so many reasons. For instance, your sexual relationship is part of the emotional glue that bonds you and keeps you close, even when you are going through a rough patch ... and nearly all couples experience rough patches at one point or another.

In this part, you'll learn all about the stages of love relationships, the importance of "generous gestures", how strong communication can enhance a couple's sex life, and the many roles of sex in a couple's relationship

The Stages of Love

In This Chapter

- ♦ What happens after the honeymoon
- ♦ Understanding the volatility of the Power Struggle Stage
- ♦ Maturing and changing both individually and as a couple
- ♦ Progressing successfully from stage to stage

As your love relationship grows, develops, and deepens over time, your dynamics, communication, feelings of intimacy, and sex life with your partner all evolve through stages. So let's open with an overview of these stages, these periods of growth and development, to give you an understanding of the big picture of the journey of love relationships.

It's an Ever Changing Landscape

Feelings of sexual desire generally ebb and flow (rather than remain fixed and constant) during the course of a long-term relationship, and shift as you transition from one phase to the next. These shifts may also be accompanied by changes (either increases or decreases) in your level of sexual desire. Within each stage, however, there are steps you can take to boost and maintain both your sex drive and level of sexual activity.

Perhaps you have heard of the TV sitcom "Til Death," which premiered in 2006 on the Fox Network. The premise of the show is that one set of neighbors (played by Brad Garrett and Joely Fischer) are "old marrieds." They still love each other in their own way, but also are chronically crabby toward each other.

A pair of newlyweds move in next door, and, not surprising, they are madly in love. In sharp contrast with the Garrett and Fischer characters, the newlyweds are still in the "honeymoon phase" of their relationship. They haven't had many or perhaps any serious disagreements yet. Nor have they said things to each other in the heat of anger that they later regret. There's no cynicism or bitterness in the way they interact with each other, just sweetness, tenderness, and adoration.

Clearly this cliché—that newlyweds are always sweet to each other while those who have been married for a time treat each other at best like comfortable old shoes and at worst like adversaries—was probably an easy pitch for the show's creators to sell to the network. Why? Because let's face it: this is an old, familiar theme that resonates with a lot of people.

So is there any truth to this widely held belief that after the honeymoon phase of a relationship comes to an end (as it must), it all goes downhill?

Not necessarily.

Experts do differ on precisely how many stages, or phases, there are in most typical love relationships. Some say eight, others say four, and so on. In this book, we are going to discuss six stages of love relationships. However, we believe that these stages are not necessarily definitive, comprehensive, or set in stone.

After all, each individual relationship is unique. Applying a strict framework to something as complicated and unquantifiable as even a typical human love relationship is far from foolproof. Nonetheless, many serious love relationships do indeed go through a series of specific, clearly defined stages. Even if some couples repeat a phase, invent a phase of their own, or skip a phase altogether, we can still talk about relationships in terms of stages. They provide a handy device for explaining the passages that many long-term couples navigate during the course of their relationship journey.

The Honeymoon Stage

True to the classic stereotype of the newlywed or newly-in-love couple, sexual desire tends to run rampant during this first stage. When two partners first get together, they experience the highly enjoyable (but, alas, temporary) "honeymoon phase" of the relationship. During this phase they have trouble keeping their hands off of each other, and all they want to do is be together every hour of every day for the rest of their lives.

In fact, it's interesting to note that some relationship experts call the honeymoon phase the *enmeshment phase*. The two lovers become so entangled (both physically and emotionally) with each other that it is almost as if they are totally enmeshed with or inseparable from one another.

For people who have just fallen in love, colors look brighter, food tastes better, and just about everything seems more beautiful and exciting than ever. They don't feel much like eating or sleeping. They want to make love and they feel euphorically happy all the time. Most love songs and romance novels are written about this raw, passionate honeymoon phase of love relationships because of its tremendous intensity, both physically and emotionally. Couples in this stage "want this feeling to last forever."

def•i•ni•tion

The **enmeshment phase** is another term for the honeymoon phase, meaning a time when two people act physically and emotionally intertwined and inseparable.

However, all things must come to an end, because change is an inevitable part of life. The honeymoon phase for couples typically lasts anywhere from six months up to two years before drawing to its inevitable conclusion, after which a continuing relationship transforms into something more comfortable and stable.

It's actually healthy and in both partners' best interest for the honeymoon phase of their relationship to come to an end. Think about it: if two people spent all of their time making love and being consumed with their own pleasure and how gloriously happy they feel about being so madly in love, they'd likely not accomplish much else for the rest of their lives. Another reason it's important for this stage to come to an end is that it can lead to silly or even irrational behavior, as well as an unhealthy denial of reality, a denial that's often referred to as "wearing rose-colored glasses."

Indeed, as exciting as this stage can be, it can also be unsettling, as if a mad scientist is tinkering with unstable chemicals in a laboratory. This stage can be so volatile and disconcerting because the sexual chemistry tends to be off the charts, giving the couple little time or emotional energy to devote to anything else. This ultimately causes neglect of the duties and responsibilities of life—another good reason for conclusion of this stage.

The Bonding or "Welcome to Reality" Stage

Transitioning out of the honeymoon phase can be difficult. After all, it is hard to say goodbye to those days of nearly constant lovemaking and gazing longingly into each other's eyes. But the next phase, which many researchers and relationship experts call the "bonding" stage or the "welcome to reality" stage, is more important to the overall health and future of a relationship than the honeymoon phase. While the honeymoon phase is known for its raw, inexhaustible passion, the bonding phase is known for the emotional comfort and security it can provide. Assuming that you and your mate have survived the often-bumpy transition out of the honeymoon phase and into the bonding stage, you'll find in this settling-down stage you still want to touch, hold, and cuddle each other, but the all-consuming need and desire to make love around the clock becomes less intense.

> **Love Booster**
>
> The "Welcome to Reality" stage is often the time when couples begin to think about starting a family, thoughts that can strongly boost their sexual desire as they actively pursue their shared dream of trying to conceive a child.

This isn't to say that your sexual energy for each other totally drops or vanishes. Far from it, hopefully! It only means that, generally, it cools down from a near-constant boiling point to a more comfortable and livable—but still constant—simmer. While you remain profoundly attracted to each other, other factors now come into play, such as a need and desire for comfort, commitment, and attachment (bonding). This bonding is emotional intimacy, and it's often found in each other in the form of meaningful conversation (more on communication later).

You and your partner were really still just getting to know each other in the honeymoon phase. You were both very likely "on your best behavior," and your *authentic selves* were probably not on display for each other very often.

But when you enter the bonding phase, you become much more comfortable and relaxed around each other. The need for any remaining pretenses or false fronts goes out the window and the two of you drop your guard, revealing more of your true, authentic selves to each other.

def•i•ni•tion

Your **authentic self** is the vulnerable, unadorned person you truly are deep inside, as opposed to the various façades you may put up in different social situations—including in the Honeymoon Stage of your love relationship.

This "welcome to reality" stage is also the place where one partner's pesky little habits, like leaving the cap off the toothpaste, can become more noticeable and bothersome to the other. In other words, this is the stage where couples come to realize that their partners are not perfect angels, but mere mortals like themselves. It's important to note that in this stage you may discover your own or your partner's sexual anxieties or inhibitions, or any embarrassment or shame (perhaps associated with past relationships) that may be affecting your relationship. (More on the subject of past relationships in Appendix B.)

With the exception of the Honeymoon Stage, which typically lasts six months to two years for most couples, we hesitate to give a specific timeframe on this second stage, or any of the remaining stages, because the lengths of each stage can vary widely from couple to couple.

The key to surviving this and all of the inevitable relationship shifts is to keep connecting and —communicating—both physically and emotionally. This requires you and your partner not take each other for granted and continue paying attention to each other, cuddling, and making love.

The Conflict or "Power Struggle" Stage

While the bonding stage helps move you from being totally enmeshed with your partner to feeling secure, settled, and connected, what you enter into next with this new breathing space is what relationship experts call a "conflict" or "power struggle" phase. Here, there can be a much greater level of fighting and yelling than you have gone through up to this point in the relationship. Some couples do not make it through this difficult phase, and the relationship ends.

But couples who manage to navigate their way through this tricky, volatile phase are generally those who work together to find ways to stay connected on an emotional and physical level despite their disagreements. They learn how to compromise, negotiate, and resolve their conflicts in healthy, nonhurtful, constructive ways (more on this in this Chapter 2.)

The power-struggle phase poses a big challenge for many couples because during this period of time they neglect their sexual relationship. A couple's spirit of cooperation may falter during this stage. Anger and frustration get in the way of their desire for intimacy with each other, and there may be less sexual mutuality and cooperation.

Mood Killer

The power struggle phase is known as a time with a great deal of disagreements and fighting between lovers, which can take its toll in the bedroom.

In addition to putting sex on the back burner, couples may also use it as a weapon against one another. For example, an angry wife may tell her husband: "If you won't agree to let me decorate the house the way I want, I won't have sex with you." And her husband may reply: "If you won't have sex with me, then you can't redecorate the house."

Power struggles like this, using sex or otherwise, is how resentments are born, and they fester and eat away at a relationship. As battles grow more heated, both partners become increasingly unhappy and resentful of each other. No one wins in a power struggle, especially a sexual one. To successfully move past this combative stage and keep the relationship alive and healthy, both partners need to learn how to communicate effectively and treat each other with respect.

As with the previous stage, we are reluctant to delineate a specific time-frame for this stage, but please know that it can take some couples several years to move successfully through this challenging phase.

Why exactly is there so much potential for conflict (or actual conflict) during this stage of the relationship? Well, a big part of the "Welcome to Reality" stage, the stage directly before this one, is in which you are no longer viewing each other through those pesky, proverbial rose-colored glasses. Whereas you were once able to overlook each other's quirks and foibles, or even consider them to be somewhat charming, by now these same foibles have grown so noticeable (and in some cases so irritating) they almost seem to glow in the dark.

Moving from honeymoon land to reality land can be quite a shock to the system. And this shock of returning to Earth can (and often does) lead to the numerous conflicts associated with this power struggle stage. At this point, both partners are trying to assert their own unique desires, tastes, wills, personalities and worldviews. It is during this complicated stage that the relationship becomes vulnerable to destruction or ripe for growth.

For example, what if two partners are only now, during the power struggle phase, discovering that they have radically different opinions on how to raise children, or how to create and maintain a household budget, or—and this point is particularly relevant for this book—how and how often they would like to make love?

As challenging and emotionally difficult as this phase can be, it can also be useful and constructive, depending in large part on how both partners handle the various disagreements that arise. In fact, many relationship experts make the argument that this stage is actually vital to a couple's survival and growth, and that without it, many relationships would stagnate, or hit an impassable wall, ultimately petering out altogether.

The key to surviving—and hopefully growing and evolving during this stage—is to remember that there are two vastly different ways to handle disagreements with one's partner (or with anybody else for that matter). The first (and most constructive) way is to handle them carefully, tactfully and with the utmost concern for the other person's feelings. The second (far more destructive) way is to do so in a rude, unkind, sarcastic, and/or bullying manner. The former gives the relationship a much greater chance of healthy survival and mutual fulfillment.

Sometimes people make the grave mistake of thinking they can be more casual—or perhaps even downright careless or hurtful—with their partner's feelings than with other people's feelings. They use unkind words, phrases or tones of voice they would never dream of using with anyone else. Perhaps you have heard the expression "You only hurt the ones you love." This sad phrase refers to the fact that people who love each other have the power to inflict significant emotional harm on one another in ways that strangers (or even mere acquaintances) never could. And, indeed, part of being a kind, mature, emotionally evolved adult is recognizing that each of us has the innate power, and choice, to do either emotional harm or good in *any* of our closest relationships—with our partners, children, parents, siblings, and friends. It behooves us, therefore, to use this great power for good as consistently as we possibly can.

For many people, the idea of a "Power Struggle" stage directly following the "Welcome to Reality" stage of a love relationship can be confusing and off-putting. However, something else to bear in mind is that when two emotionally healthy partners start to bicker, butt heads and jockey for position, they are not actually fighting for emotional dominance over the other. Rather, they are struggling mightily to achieve an *equal balance of power*—a balance that feels natural, comfortable, healthy and right to both of them. This process can take some time, some negotiating and often some renegotiating further down the road as well.

When two partners finally achieve the laudable goal of a satisfyingly equal balance of power, their relationship will ripen and deepen. This isn't to say that they will never argue again once they have moved past the power struggle. It is just that toward the end of this important phase, they will likely have reached a preliminary agreement (or a set of preliminary agreements) about certain fundamental points, agreements that can then serve as useful reference points, or emotional cushions, during later moments of tension or disharmony.

Of course, the agreements reached during this stage are not set in stone, which means it's essential for both partners to remain flexible and open to renegotiation and compromise throughout the course of their relationship. Since this is a book about sexual desire, let's use an example keyed to this topic. During the honeymoon phase, it is common for both partners to feel a huge surge of sexual desire. However, during the welcome to reality stage or the power struggle stage, it may become evident for the first time that one partner has a higher (and in some cases a much higher) level of sexual desire than the other.

Many sex experts, including therapist and "divorce-buster" Michele Weiner-Davis, have devoted large portions of their careers to exploring such differences. They have noted that the way two partners handle their different levels of sexual desire can end up making or breaking their relationship.

Why is it so important for couples to work on bridging the gaps in their sexual desire? In her books and articles, Weiner-Davis continually reminds us that sex is important in any intimate relationship, and of course sex feels like a particularly urgent and pressing need for the partner who craves it the most.

When the higher-desire partner feels rebuffed and rejected too often, and the lower-desire partner feels excessively nagged for sex, resentments start to build on both sides. Perhaps most important of all, as Weiner-Davis and other experts point out, the struggle over sex and intimate touch combined with both partners' mounting resentments can lead to a distancing effect and an unfortunate drop in intimacy on all levels. More specifically, kissing, intimate talking, snuggling, cuddling, joking, flirting, teasing and connecting can also start to fade away along with the sex.

When the sexual and emotional intimacies drain out of a couple's relationship, these losses may herald the beginning of the end. Or, it may serve as the couple's wake-up call, the realization that something has got to give for the relationship to recover and for both partners to find happiness.

Some couples seem to grasp intuitively the importance of compromising or meeting in the middle as an emotionally healthy, highly effective means of resolving these sorts of conflicts. Other couples need to learn more about flexibility and the art of compromise to keep their intimate lives on track.

Many who seek couples therapy are struggling with a discrepancy in their level of sexual desire, so if you and your partner are facing this problem, it's important for you to know that you are not alone. Also, while it is mostly women who report the feeling of low sexual desire to their doctors and/or therapists, men, too, can struggle with low desire.

Men are often reluctant to talk about this issue, in large part because of societal pressure and stereotype of macho men, who are depicted as always wanting sex.

This topic of a gap in sexual desire is one we will be revisiting throughout the book, because it is such a key component of any serious discussion about enhancing sexual desire. But for now, if you and your partner are among the many couples in the United States and throughout the world who are currently engaged in what could fairly be described as a power struggle over the gap in your levels of sexual desire, see Appendix B for helpful tips and strategies specific to this issue.

One dictionary definition of "regrouping" is "reorganizing for a renewed effort after a temporary setback." And certainly for couples who survive the power struggle phase, they are putting themselves in the great position to regroup on their relationship. They have put each other (and themselves) to the ultimate relationship test exposing their own fears and foibles, their strengths and weaknesses, mostly through anger and strife.

When partners have endured and, most important, successfully conquered or gotten past a particularly stressful power struggle over sex, they often find their sexual desire for each other is once again on the rise. And this brings them to the next stage in their relationship, often referred to as the regrouping or reevaluation phase.

More frequent and more enjoyable lovemaking is often a hallmark of this phase, as partners rediscover why they fell in love in the first place.

Let's examine more closely why both partners' sexual desire (as well as their frequency of lovemaking), can increase during this stage. For starters, it can feel awfully good just to survive the power struggle phase as an intact couple.

Secondly, if one of the issues fought about during the power struggle phase happened to be differing levels of sexual desire, a couple may have managed to bridge their desire gap by arriving at a compromise that feels fair and satisfying to both of them.

Thirdly, when couples successfully work through a difficult time, they often feel, rightly so, they have accomplished a significant goal. And this sense of accomplishment often serves as a potent aphrodisiac, boosting both partners' sense of self-esteem as well as their levels of sexual desire.

During this regrouping phase, many couples find they can calm down and relax after the tumult and bickering of the power struggle phase. They are also regaining strength and catching their second wind in preparation for the all-important next phase of "individuation."

But for other couples, the "Regrouping or Reevaluation Stage" can lead to a serious reconsideration of their relationship. Rather than picking each other up and dusting each other off, they ask themselves whether they want to stay together at all in the aftermath of their power-struggle-related conflicts.

In other words, this can be a time when one or both partners may find themselves taking a step back in an attempt to more objectively decide if the relationship is actually worth continuing. Sometimes, if the power struggle phase went on for too long, if the disharmony and fighting of that phase only led to more disharmony and more fighting, the couple may ultimately decide that this is an appropriate time to end the relationship rather than stay together.

The Individuation and Reunification Stage

If the relationship survives the reevaluation phase, the two partners will likely emerge from it feeling more strongly unified than ever. And once two partners regroup and feel fully and happily bonded with each other, they can comfortably and confidently start to individuate, meaning they move into the "individuation" or "reunification" stage of their relationship. They feel deeply committed as a team of two, and at the same time feel like fully realized individuals.

In this stage, both partners feel connected not only to each other, but also to their own powerful feelings of individuality. Passions and interests may not be the same for both partners, but the relationship with each other remains the home base or touchstone even as they each feel contented and fulfilled as individuals, and supported as such.

Individuation can have a potent effect on sexual desire, because two partners who feel whole and fulfilled independently bring a lot more to the table when it comes to their sex life. People who feel happy as individuals tend to have more confidence, and these happy, fulfilled, confident people tend to approach all aspects of their lives—including their sex lives—with more gusto.

Therefore, this individuation stage of a love relationship is also termed the reunification phase, because it can include within it a lovemaking-filled second-honeymoon phase. The reason this can happen is partly because both partners are feeling independently happy and confident, and partly because they are spending just enough time together and just enough time apart in their own pursuits to more fully appreciate each other. This combination can help rekindle the sparks and the sense of newness and excitement that partners felt during their initial honeymoon phase.

> **Love Booster**
>
> The Individuation and Reunification Stage gives both partners a much needed opportunity to simultaneously exercise their personal autonomy and bolster their sense of unity—a winning combination that can send sexual desire sky-rocketing.

A helpful visual aid is to think of a first honeymoon as two half circles coming together to form one enmeshed circle. Then, by way of contrast, think of a second honeymoon as two fully realized and differentiated whole circles coming together, overlapping but not enmeshed. "Being your own person"—rather than being an enmeshed half of a pair—can be a real turn-on, both for your partner and for yourself! It makes you even sexier and more desirable to each other, and this can most certainly boost sexual desire.

The Unconditional Love and Acceptance Stage

Once couples feel secure as independent individuals in their relationship, having gained strength and knowledge all along the way in the stages prior, they cross over to a final stage, the unconditional love and acceptance stage, where their love is just that, unconditional, and they are fully accepting of each other.

In this final stage, a couple's enduring love translates into lovemaking (regardless of frequency or intensity) that is nearly always a tender, affectionate expression of these mutual feelings of love and acceptance. Sex in this stage is fueled with desire driven by factors far different than those of earlier stages.

Generally speaking, this final stage comes later in most relationships (and later in the lives of both partners), although some exceptional couples may reach it an earlier point in their lives. While the lovemaking during this final stage may not necessarily fall into the "tearing each other's clothes off" category, what it may lack in terms of physical acrobatics it more than makes up for in terms of deeply satisfying emotional content.

Many relationship experts believe that only a small portion of couples make it all the way to this final stage, just as many of us do not possess the emotional wherewithal to become fully *self-actualized* human beings during the course of our lifetimes. However, we like to say "Keep your eyes on the prize," and we advise couples to focus on the possibility that you and your partner can end up being one of those couples who manage to achieve this highly sought after, deeply freeing and satisfying goal.

def•i•ni•tion

Self-actualization is a psychological term coined by the American psychologist Abraham Maslow as the pinnacle of a pyramid he described as the human "hierarchy of needs." It refers to the achievement of one's full potential through creativity, independence, morality, sophisticated problem-solving skills, spontaneity, open-mindedness, a lack of prejudice, and a profound understanding of the factual workings of "the real world."

All of the stages we explained in the chapter are, quite simply, the journey of love, and every relationship progresses, even regresses, at its own pace. As you'll learn in this book, communication, commitment, and perseverance are keys to successfully moving through the various stages of love and keeping your sexual desire for one another alive all along the way.

The Least You Need to Know

◆ Nearly all couples go through a series of well-defined stages of relationship development and growth that can be predicted with a fair degree of accuracy.

◆ The Honeymoon phase is a temporary state of a budding relationship known for lots of excitement, passion, and sex.

◆ Disagreements and fighting are common in the Power Struggle phase as couples see more of the realities of their partner and relationship, such as differing levels of sexual desire.

◆ The timeframe for each stage various from couple to couple, and some may skip a stage or fall back to a previous one at some point in their relationship.

◆ Communication and commitment are key for couples to survive the various love relationship stages and their transitions.

2

The Link Between Sex and Intimacy

In This Chapter

- ◆ The important role of sexual generosity in your love life
- ◆ Sex as a means of communication with your partner
- ◆ Ways flirting can keeps your sexual fires burning
- ◆ How improving your communication skills can improve your sex life

An engaging, satisfying and fulfilling sex life is something we all want, need and crave. Intimacy, in particular, refers to the close bond or deep sense of sharing and connectedness that loving couples experience with each other. It is based on love, respect, belief in each other, and a powerful mutual concern for each other's overall health and well-being. The bond of intimacy that exists between two long-term partners or spouses needs to be consistently nurtured for it to grow and flourish over the course of time. Also, in any long-term, committed relationship or marriage, the link between sexual intimacy and emotional intimacy is a powerful one. So when you feel particularly close to your partner on an emotional level, this can significantly enhance your feelings of sexual desire.

A big part of feeling a strong sexual and emotional connection with your partner has to do with maintaining strong communication. Perhaps you have noticed (in your own and other relationships) that couples who have been together for a significant period of time tend to develop a sort of "shorthand" with each other. They know each other so well they are often able to finish each other's sentences, or to convey complex messages to each other in a single, meaningful glance.

This chapter explores various ways in which couples express themselves —communicate—both verbally and nonverbally with each other. We'll look at how a strong communication link can enhance your feelings of emotional and physical intimacy, which can, in turn, enhance your sexual desire.

Just Between Us

Now that you have an understanding of the various stages of love relationships, let's turn our focus to the sexual, exclusive dynamics of two committed partners.

For monogamous couples, sex is the one activity that you engage in exclusively with your significant other and no one else. This exclusivity adds to its sacredness and makes it an essential part of your bond with each other. Your bond is comprised of many key components in addition to sex, such as love, commitment, friendship, trust, compatibility, faithfulness, respect, support, appreciation, and shared dreams and goals, to name just a few.

So each time you and your partner make love, you are not only being satisfied and connected on a physical level, you are also reaffirming and strengthening all of the components of your relationship. Moreover, the bond you have with your partner is strengthened and consistently reinforced also by

> **" Notable Quotable**
>
> "True love needs the foundation of physical affection. Bodies not only house our spirits, they express our spirits. They communicate, without words, the essence of our beings."
>
> —Daphne Rose Kingma, author of *True Love: How To Make Your Relationship Sweeter, Deeper, and More Passionate*

having loving, intimate conversations. Each embrace with your beloved partner can feel like a mini-homecoming.

Sexual Chemistry

The "spark" or sexual chemistry that exists between two lovers is somewhat mysterious. But, what's not so puzzling is that sexual chemistry and compatibility are definitely important to any marriage or long-term relationship. One of the many messages you convey when you make love is that you find your partner as sexually appealing now as ever, and without that, a relationship isn't bound to last—at least not in a sexually satisfying way.

Yet we don't fully understand why two particular people have a spark, fall in love, and stay in love.

Research on the "rules of attraction" has produced some interesting findings. For instance, some scientists (particularly evolutionary psychologists) maintain that many of us are sexually drawn to partners with symmetrical facial features. They believe this is Mother Nature's way of guiding us toward healthy, attractive mates, with whom we can have healthy, attractive children.

On a similar note, a recent study about attraction conducted at Aberdeen University in the United Kingdom concluded that women like men who are smiled at by others, particularly other women.

> **Notable Quotable**
>
> "What stimulates the sexual appetite is sometimes puzzling. Sweet sex grows out of approval and acceptance and harmony."
> —William Ashoka Ross, author of *The Wonderful Little Sex Book*

> **Notable Quotable**
>
> On sexual chemistry: "If the married sex fire seems to go out, stir, blow, and add more flammables."
> —Dr. Max Vogt, www.MarriageBlueprint.com

Scientific studies such as these reveal some generalities about what people find attractive in potential mates. But what they can't reveal are the reasons you find your particular partner so sexy and appealing to you. For whatever combination of reasons (and there are many), when the two of you first met, you both felt that unmistakable pull of raw physical attraction that lies at the heart of sexual chemistry. And fortunately, there are ways to continually renew those feelings and keep tapping into that sexual chemistry you felt during your "honeymoon phase."

The Generous Gesture

You've heard the sage old saying, "It's better to give than receive." Truer words have never been spoken (or written) when it comes to sex in a relationship. In fact, many people involved in loving, committed relationships find the selfless act of giving their partners physical and emotional pleasure totally rewarding. This kind of sex, in which both partners are more concerned with their partners' pleasure than with their own, can be particularly fulfilling on many levels.

It's likely not surprising that sex (or the lack thereof) is one of the major issues that drives couples to seek marital counseling. For example, this true success story perfectly illustrates the power of generous gestures in love relationships: Marian and Jim, both in their late 40s, sought counseling when their 12-year-old marriage was turning sour. They loved each other and greatly enjoyed parenting their 7-year-old son, but their relationship was in a slump and they didn't know how to pull themselves out. Neither felt understood or appreciated by the other.

They fought over chores, the budget, what color to paint the bathroom, and so on. Their sex life was nonexistent. Marian was tired when she came home from work and not in the mood for sex. She had dinner to cook and household chores to finish. Jim would rather have sex than help with chores. And so they were locked in the battle of: "If you won't do for me, I won't do for you." They were living like roommates and not happy in their relationship.

One day driving home from work, Marian had the epiphany that if she gave Jim what he said he wanted (sex), that maybe she'd get what she wanted in return (help). So that evening, rather than immediately cleaning up the kitchen after dinner, Marian seduced Jim instead. She realized when she gave Jim the sex he needed, that she actually needed it, too.

And it probably won't surprise you that Jim started doing his share of the chores.

As simple as the notion may seem, it can be a difficult one to act on, but is well worth the effort with extremely satisfying rewards.

Being Lovers and Friends

It is wonderful to be best friends with your partner, but to be best friends and lovers is the ultimate. Couples who are both are satisfied and fulfilled over the long haul.

Remember that your friendship and your sexual relationship go hand-in-hand. They work together to keep your intimate bond going strong, and you will find it easier to use kind, loving, supportive words—as you would for your best friend—and to use your loving touch and your eyes

 Love Booster

Couples who share all forms of intimacy, including friendship and sexual intimacy, are continually reinforcing their bonds of love and companionship. Their lovemaking enhances and nourishes their friendship, and vice versa.

(lots of eye contact)—as you would for your lover—to convey just how much you care for each other, both as lovers and as best friends.

Expressing Your Sexual Self

Couples use sex to communicate and express themselves to each other, both verbally and nonverbally. Often, partners nonverbally express sexuality by dressing in a seductive manner, or by wearing their hair and make-up in a special way. They might also use certain facial expressions, body language, gestures and mannerisms to express desire to make love. For instance, they might wink, beckon, raise their eyebrows, or smile at their lovers in a naughty, "come hither" fashion.

Making love enables you to reveal your different moods and feelings. A tough day at the office or an emotional event may be expressed to your partner in your desire for gentle, tender sex, or an action-packed day or lively experience may extend to wildly passionate sex, and every possible shade of gray in between, given the mood. The type of love you make with your partner can be a big indicator of the emotions you are feeling at the time.

For instance, if you are feeling excited about an accomplishment, you may end up expressing that excitement by making particularly wild and passionate love to your partner later that night, or in whatever fashion is expressive of you and what you're feeling.

Moreover, saying the words "I love you" (the verbal expression of emotional intimacy) and making love (the physical expression of emotional intimacy) are two different but equally important ways to show your partner exactly how much you care.

> **Notable Quotable** _____
>
> "Let your bodies speak your truth. Make love with the consciousness that your body can say what you cannot, and know that in its sensuous abandon, sexual passion is the dancing of the spirit."
>
> —Daphne Rose Kingma, author of _True Love: How to Make Your Relationship Sweeter, Deeper, and More Passionate_

Think of your sex life as a significant portion of an ongoing conversation that you have been having with your partner since the day you met ... and that you hope will go on forevermore. It's good to keep in mind that intellectual stimulation and sexual stimulation are inextricably linked, and stimulating conversation that isn't about sex is really a part of foreplay. Talking with your partner about things that interest you both, whether it's politics, current events, a movie, a book, or even the weather, is a way to express and stimulate sexual desire. After all, stimulating conversation is a great form of foreplay!

Crossing the Communication Divide

Learning to communicate lovingly and effectively with your partner is essential for the sex and emotional-intimacy link to exist between the two of you. According to research, women use communication largely to bond and nurture, while men use it mainly to compete or express feelings of independence.

Linguist Deborah Tannen, the author of _You Just Don't Understand_, talks extensively in her work about these differences. She pays special attention to the ways men and women hear and process language. Tannen and other experts observe that from boyhood on, men are often taught to view just about everything (even conversation) as a competition, an opportunity for one-upmanship. In stark contrast, from girlhood on, women are often raised to view the bulk of their social interactions as opportunities to foster closeness and emotional intimacy.

Thus, men and women often take different approaches to and interpretations of conversation, and they expect to achieve radically different goals when they communicate. This can make them feel as if, quite literally, they are speaking in different languages. These differences can cause marital conflict unless they are acknowledged and addressed by both partners and there is willingness to compromise and seek common ground.

But crossing the communication divide is not as hard as it may sound. Here are some tips to help you along the way.

The Power of Empathy

An enlightening tool for communicating is learning how to empathize with your partner. Try putting yourself in your partner's shoes in order to see and experience your sexual relationship from the other point of view. Getting the other perspective gives you an understanding of how your sex life is experienced from the other side, and gives you the opportunity to communicate more effectively, knowing how the other side feels. Ask yourself if you are fully enjoying your sex life, and if your partner is, too. What is the attitude toward sex? Healthy, fulfilling sexuality enables both partners to enjoy sexual pleasure.

Consistently empathizing with each other can make communicating so much easier. Partners who genuinely empathize with each other more often than not are the most successful at finding common ground, solving any problems that may arise (including sexual problems), and keeping their bonds of emotional and physical intimacy going strong.

def•i•ni•tion

Empathy is the ability to put yourself in another person's shoes in order to fully imagine exactly how that other person is feeling in a given situation. When people have the capacity to empathize with others, they understand them at a deeper level and are better emotionally equipped both to feel compassion for them and to meet their needs.

Use your powers of empathy to tune into each other's sexual needs and desires, as well as each other's concerns, inhibitions, and worries. This way you will know that you are on the same page, sexually speaking. And this powerful feeling of connection can have a wonderfully bolstering effect on your sexual desire.

Common Ground and Compromise

When two partners value and recognize the need for strong communication (particularly when it comes to sex and other potentially sensitive subjects), chances are they will be able to find common ground and compromise, no matter what obstacles they face.

For instance, if a husband says he wants sex in the middle of the night and his wife says she'd rather have it in the morning, first of all they both want sex, so they are already on common ground; and second, rather than arguing about something they both want, they can compromise to have sex earlier in the evening or whenever they both agree to. Perhaps it's the middle of the night sometimes, and in the morning other times.

> **Love Booster**
>
> Particularly with sex, mastering the art of compromise with your partner—mutual concession and agreement—will enhance feelings of sexual desire for you both, because the end result is that you each get something you want and need.

If you and your partner are seeking understanding and compromise in your communication, then it's much easier to get your sex life back on track.

Commitment to the Goal

Couples who want to maintain or even improve their sexual desire and communication need to become and remain committed to the process, and can do so in a variety of ways. For instance, they can promise each other they are both "in this for the long haul," and they both understand that sexual desire may ebb and flow over time but they are both determined to explore what will work for them—all the specific tricks and techniques—in terms of boosting mutual desire. Of course, lovemaking is a major way two longtime partners demonstrate and reinforce their commitment and communication bond with each other. But commitment comes in other forms as well, that really lay the groundwork for enhanced sexual desire. Some of the other ways include stimulating conversation, sharing good times and laughter, creating memories together, sharing quality time with children and other family members, enjoying good meals together, traveling together, watching movies, and taking long walks.

Also, believe it or not, many couples bond and feel commitment through performing the most routine, tedious daily tasks together, such as running errands, or taking care of household chores. In other words, just about any task that two partners undertake *together* can double as a bonding opportunity and expression of commitment. Granted, writing bills together may not be nearly as romantic or as much fun as making love, but any task that you perform as a dynamic duo (rather than solo) can make you feel closer and more connected.

Practical Communication Tips

Strong communication fosters a peaceful home environment, and a happy, loving household is the foundation of all great intimate relationships. Communicating with your partner about sex, or any other important topic, ultimately comes down to mastering some pretty basic and practical but very necessary skills.

Are You Listening?

It is normal for you and your partner occasionally to experience a disparity in your sexual desire. Sometimes one partner wants to hug, kiss, and cuddle without having sex, while the other is intent on "going all the way." The ability to talk and listen to each other's wishes and desires is paramount if you want to keep your sexual fires burning bright.

When it comes to sex and intimacy, remember that lovemaking is all about being in tune with one another. Getting in tune includes listening, especially active listening. And because active listening is so very important to your communication about sex—and to every other topic under the sun, for that matter—we're going to break it down and discuss it in some detail.

Active listening does not mean you always have to agree with your partner; it means you are paying particularly close attention to his words with the intent of gaining a firm understanding of where he is coming from.

Let your partner know you are actively listening by using generous, engaged body language such as leaning in closer, making direct eye contact, and nodding frequently. Also restate, in your words, or just summarize what he has said to let him know that you heard the message.

When there's a pause for a breath or a natural stopping point, ask questions about what he is telling you. This affirms further that not only are you grasping what he is saying, but also that you understand and empathize with his point of view (even if you do not agree with it completely).

Also let your mate know you are open to having future conversations about the topic at hand, if need be, as part of your larger, never-ending, ongoing conversation. It is such a fundamental part of your relationship as a couple.

If something comes up later that relates to your earlier discussion, say something like: "This reminds me of what you were saying before ..." This is a clear signal you were actively listening in the initial conversation, and that you value thoughts and opinions so much that you remember them, think about them, and even apply them to other situations throughout your day.

When you listen to your partner in an empathetic, "putting-yourself-in-their-shoes" way, does not feel judged or criticized, but rather safe and supported. She knows with total confidence that her deep, innermost thoughts and feelings can be revealed to you and that you will never look at her askance, or roll your eyes, or think she is silly or foolish for feeling a certain way. This security, in turn, enables a partner to always be her truest, fully realized self when in your presence.

When the two of you feel you can be your most authentic selves with each other, inhibitions will fall away, making your love life more exciting and fulfilling than ever.

Once again, keep in mind that understanding and accepting your partner for who he is and how he feels is not the same as agreeing with all of his opinions or feelings. When you and your partner feel truly heard, understood, and fully supported by each other, your sexual and emotional desire for one another will increase exponentially.

Everyone Loves a Flirt

Think back to how the two of you met. Maybe it was at a party, through a mutual friend, in line at the post office, or in the park while walking your dog.

Whatever the circumstances of your first meeting and the early days of your relationship, flirting was certainly part of the fun and the attraction. Maybe it was a wink, a soft touch to your face, or a hand on your knee that lingered just a beat or two longer than necessary. Whatever specific form your mutual flirting took, you were letting each other know you found each other hot, sexy, and off-the-charts desirable.

What's so great about flirting is that it can be as fresh and exciting in a later stage of your relationship as it was when you first met. Flirting now communicates that same, all-important message that it conveyed back then: "I find you incredibly sexy, and I want to rip off all your clothes and make love with you right this minute!"

Some people say that flirting is a lost art form. But this doesn't need to be the case in your relationship! If the amount of flirting in your relationship has declined in recent months or years, make it your mission right now to revive this saucy, exciting practice.

After all, not only is flirting enjoyable in its own right, but it can also be a natural and exciting lead-in to lovemaking. So be aware that with every flirtatious gesture, you are sending a sexy message about what may be happening later on.

Flirt by nuzzling your partner's neck, calling him "Baby," paying him a genuine compliment, sharing a hardy laugh with him, rubbing his shoulders, pressing your body up against his, or writing a little love note. This is active and loving flirting.

And you had better believe that he will love every minute of it! In fact, he will lap up all the attention and adoration like a little puppy dog. After all, your flirting with him makes him feel sexy, manly, valued, and totally loved. And who wouldn't like to feel that way?

Flirting is essential to enhancing your sexual desire because it keeps your relationship bouncy, light, playful, and joyous rather than heavy, dour, or overly serious. Not only that, flirting is easy, and costs absolutely nothing, yet is one of the most important emotional investments you can make in your relationship ... because it can result in such wonderful dividends!

Actually, flirting when you have been together for years may be even more important than the flirting that you did when you first met. After all, flirting and making love were almost the only two things that you did back in the honeymoon phase of your relationship! The trick, of course, is to continue finding a variety of exciting, wonderful ways to flirt with each other and engage each other's full attention years and years after the honeymoon phase has come and gone.

Love Booster

For a fascinating glimpse into the art and science of flirting, read (or watch the movie) *Memoirs of A Geisha*. Geishas were not prostitutes, but they were peerless flirts. With their attention to detail, their beautiful make-up and kimonos, and their talents as brilliant conversationalists, they raised flirting to the level of an art form.

Let Your Fingers Do the Talking

It's time to focus specifically on all the joys—and the very real relationship benefits—of communicating nonverbally with your partner. Every time you hug and kiss your partner hello or goodbye, or hold hands while walking down the street, or give her a little scratch on the back or a massage, you are conveying the wonderful two-fold message that you love her as much as ever, and that you would never take her—or the love that the two of you share—for granted.

Kissing, cuddling, hugging, massaging, scratching, and even tickling are all wonderful, tactile ways to let your partner know that you love him madly, you still find him eminently touchable, and you want to be with him for the long haul.

And if you would like him to touch you more often, make sure you let him know it in a variety of ways. Don't hesitate to ask for a brief back-rub, for instance, or to link your arm through his when you are walking down the street.

As we've said, all of these small but loving gestures build upon each other bit by bit, helping your emotional bond with your partner continue to grow and flourish. And remember, everything you do to continually strengthen your bond of emotional intimacy can help keep your feelings of sexual desire going strong as well.

Handling Disagreements Effectively

It's not exactly a state secret that arguing and fighting can have a very negative effect on your sex life.

The first thing to remember is that everyone experiences feelings of anger—every person in every relationship. Feeling angry from time to time is perfectly natural and understandable, but *acting* enraged toward your partner (or anyone else) is totally unacceptable.

For most, anger does not stimulate desire, but rather detracts from it. So if anger is an ongoing issue with you or your partner, consider counseling in order to work through it and move on. If you blow your stack once in a while, it's important to know that all is not lost. But it's absolutely essential to apologize when you lose your cool with your partner. If you both keep your cool most of the time, then losing your temper on occasion—while certainly unfortunate—is also forgivable.

Fortunately, there are several effective ways to prevent minor, or even major, disagreements from snowballing into massive, earth-shattering, often-regret-ridden fights.

Take Five

While easier said than done, one simple way to stop a disagreement from escalating is to remove yourself from the situation for as long as necessary. Taking a breather enables you to gather your wits about you before you say something you may later come to regret. You can always resume the conversation at a future point, after you have both had the chance to calm down.

Try to ask yourself: "What am I angry about?" Are you disappointed or hurt? Sometimes anger is a deep expression of frustration over the lack of sex, and possibly has nothing to do with the situation at hand. Unresolved hurts and disappointments will put out the sexual fire. If your relationship has become a battleground rather than your safe haven, chances are your sexual desire has decreased as well. Sometimes anger (and the decrease in sexual desire that can accompany it), is masking other issues, such as a fear of achieving true intimacy with your partner. In this case, ask yourself if you, and/or your partner, are picking fights all the time to push each other away.

> **Mood Killer**_____
>
> Leave criticisms out of your lovemaking. When the timing is right, by all means, stick up for yourself and negotiate your disagreements, but don't use sex as a bargaining tool.

Stay Focused

Keeping your conversation totally focused on the particular subject, and nothing else, is another technique to keep a disagreement from swelling. Don't allow the conversation to veer off into unrelated, potentially unresolved emotional territory.

For instance, let's say that you received two invitations for two different events on the same Saturday, and you and your partner are having trouble agreeing on which event to attend. Don't bring other unrelated subjects into this conversation, such as who has been doing or not doing things around the house. Instead focus all of your attention on this particular Saturday and the two events in question.

Compromise and Be Respectful

In disagreements, there are two outcomes: one of you changes your mind, or you find a way to compromise. For instance, if the two Saturday events in question are not many miles apart, maybe the two of you can put in an appearance at both.

It is also important in argument, and at all times, to keep your tone of voice soft and gentle and the words you choose as positive and life-affirming as possible. For instance, "I understand that you feel sad about not being able to attend Event A, and when I put myself in your shoes, I can certainly see why you feel that way. But what if we put our heads together, and try to figure out a way to go to both events?"

It's inevitable you and your partner will disagree from time to time; it's just the nature of life, people, and relationships. But you should always strive to "fight clean" and treat each other with respect and tender loving care—even when you disagree. Make that *especially* when you disagree! You will be doing yourselves a huge favor, not only in terms of your love life, but also in terms of the overall health of your relationship.

Notable Quotable

"Arguing and sex have an inverse relationship to each other. The more arguing, the less good sex. Fight if you need to—a good fight clears out a lot of muck and gets fresh energy moving—but for goodness sakes, don't niggle … don't harp or quibble. Don't debate. Nit-picking is one big turn-off."

—William Ashoka Ross, author of The *Wonderful Little Sex Book*

After all, when it comes to expressing anger, no one likes a drama queen (or a drama king, for that matter). Keep the over-the-top theatrics and fireworks out of your argument … and save them for your sex life!

One other brief point about disagreements to note is your relationship isn't meant to be a game of one-upmanship. Your disagreements aren't battles to be won or lost, in which only one of you can emerge victorious. Every disagreement presents the two of you with a fresh opportunity to work together toward a compromise that you can both live with and enjoy.

Mood Killer

If you are feeling irritated about something, ask yourself: "Do I really need to say this right now?" When the two of you are thinking about getting intimate, nothing kills a mood quite as quickly as a scolding, sarcasm, disapproval, or a mean word thrown like a knife.

If you put your heads together, you'll find that there is almost always a third option that can satisfy you both. Relationships require support, nurturing, a constant flow of giving and taking, a shared willingness to accommodate each other's wishes, and a mutual desire to find common ground, or what some people call a middle path. Sometimes, when you aren't seeing eye to eye about something, it may take you a while to reach that common ground, but with effort and determination, you can and will get there.

To review for a moment, your main communication goals as a couple are to deepen emotional intimacy, show affection, enhance sexual desire and pleasure, and actively listen to and empathize with each other.

Love Booster

Fight fairly and respectfully, and don't mix fighting with your sexual connection. Forgive freely and let go of grudges so that you don't go to sleep angry. If you set aside disagreements, sexual passion is bound to bubble up in the bedroom.

As you work on reinforcing the sexual and emotional intimacy links that keep the two of you close, remember to use your skills of compromise and negotiation to resolve your disagreements amicably. When the two of you achieve these goals, not only are you creating a loving relationship and household for yourselves and your family—which is a worthy goal in its own right—but you are also paving the way to a deeply fulfilling sex life!

The Least You Need to Know

◆ Sexual desire can ebb and flow throughout the course of a relationship, but it is possible to enhance sexual desire at any time and make your sexual connection more satisfying. Being affectionate and loving is the first step toward increasing sexual desire.

◆ Sex is a big part of the uniquely close and intimate link that you share with your partner and no one else. Because sex is just for the two of you, this makes it a particularly sacred, intimate, and precious part of your relationship as a couple.

◆ The two of you are constantly communicating in a variety of verbal and nonverbal ways, so it is helpful to hone your communications skills to keep your sexual relationship—and your relationship as a whole—going strong.

◆ Healthy communication of all kinds is key to any strong love relationship, but sex itself is an important form of communication partners use to express their innermost thoughts and feelings to one another throughout every stage of their relationship.

◆ Flirting and touching are two important methods that long-term couples use to convey their mutual appreciation of and love for one another.

Chapter 3

The Many Roles of Sex in Your Life

In This Chapter

- ◆ Lovemaking takes on many wonderful, varied roles in your relationship with your partner
- ◆ Sex is one way loving adult partners "play" with each other
- ◆ Stress relief is a major role of sex in your relationship
- ◆ Making love with your partner is a great form of exercise
- ◆ Spiritual connection is a role of sex for some couples

To enhance sexual desire, it can be helpful (and also quite exciting) to think about all the wonderful roles that sex can play, not only in your lives as individuals, but also in your relationship as a couple.

In Chapter 2, we talked at length about how sex can bring partners closer on an emotional level. We discussed the powerful connection between sexual intimacy and emotional intimacy, and how each continually nourishes and enhances the other.

Because sexual desire and emotional intimacy are so powerfully and inextricably linked, the closer you feel to your partner (emotionally speaking), the more you want to make love. And vice versa: the more you have sex, the closer you will feel on an emotional level.

But actually, deepening your bond of emotional intimacy is just one of many roles that sex plays in your lives together. In this chapter, we will explore the *other* roles of sex in your relationship. When you take a closer look at all of these roles, you gain an even greater appreciation of the magnitude of your sexual relationship with your partner, which can further enhance your sexual desire and overall enjoyment of sex.

Let's Play!

When you were a kid, no one ever had to remind you to play. You instinctively wanted to do it, and knew it was the number-one item on your agenda all day every day.

But once we grow up and assume our adult roles in life, we often forget how important it is to still play and enjoy ourselves each and every day. After all, adults need some relief from the stress and pressures of their work lives and their many other responsibilities. Play and recreation activities of all kinds, including lovemaking with their partners, can provide them with the healthy, creative, stress-reducing and life-affirming outlet they need to stay in touch with the joyful side of life.

Love Booster

Thinking of sex with your partner as recess or free play time for adults can stimulate playfulness in your sexual desire.

Couples who strive to keep sex a big part of the "play" in their lives are actually making a wonderful emotional investment in their relationship and in themselves. A playful sexual spirit gives you a portable sense of pleasure you can carry with you at all times. It's important to understand the various aspects of sex as play and how to bring back this playful side of you if you and/or your partner have lost it.

Sex is one of the greatest forms of play a couple can experience together, and you can do it in a number of ways suited to what you and your partner enjoy.

Bedroom Antics

How can you bring the spirit of play into your bedroom?

First, remember to laugh! Sex does not need to be serious business all the time. Quite the opposite. It can be full of joy, playfulness and exuberance. There is even room for some teasing and silliness in the bedroom, particularly as the two of you are getting started, before you ease your way into more passionate activity. Talk about some silly things, have a pillow fight or play a sexual game to bring out your fun sides and lighten the atmosphere.

Notable Quotable

"Whoever called it necking was a poor judge of anatomy."

—Groucho Marx

Notable Quotable

"Sexiness wears thin after a while and beauty fades, but to be married to a man who makes you laugh every day, ah, now that's a real treat."

—Joanne Woodward

Secondly, getting in touch with your playful side in the bedroom involves creativity, curiosity and a willing spirit with sex. For instance, your sex play with your partner can include trying out new sexual techniques in playful fashion, or getting dressed up in risqué outfits that makes you feel playful, sexy and amorous, and that also turn on your partner.

Just Have Fun with It

Fun sex is created through a light-hearted, adventurous, willing, spontaneous, and non-self-conscious approach. This playful orientation makes sex with your partner something the two of you will want to keep coming back for more of!

Remember, sex doesn't always need to be analyzed in depth. In fact, more often than not, sex with your partner can just be, well … sex! In other words, rather than overthinking your love life, why not just sit back and enjoy it for the pleasurable, playful activity that it is?

Of course, we live in a self-analytical age. We have a tendency to scrutinize just about every aspect of our lives, including our sex lives. But needless difficulties can arise when you look for deeper meanings in your partner's every statement or action. Remember that many offhand statements and actions have no hidden meanings whatsoever, so why drive yourself crazy looking for them?

> **Mood Killer**
>
> Nothing can ruin a romantic evening faster than bringing up a super-serious subject right before getting intimate.

The Woody Allen movie *Annie Hall* is a perfect example of overthinking sex. In the film, the characters analyze their sex lives endlessly, and their incessant chatter drives them to needless neuroses and sexual hang-ups. They nearly stop enjoying sex altogether because their nonstop analysis of it sucks the joy and playfulness right out of one of life's most enjoyable pastimes!

Fortunately, and quite fittingly, *Annie Hall* is a comedy that reminds us that sex can be fun, playful and even downright silly at times and not to take it too seriously or it will take all the fun and play right out of it.

Have fun with it, be playful in it, and enjoy it … that's what it's there for!

Dance with Me

Sex is a lot like dancing—they are both aerobic, energizing activities as well as sources of physical and emotional connection. Dancing is a way to bring out the playful and very sensual sides of you and your partner, making it an excellent source of play for sex. It can be fast and light-hearted or slow and sexy depending on the mood … just like sex. Whatever type of dancing you're into or would be willing to try, be it ballroom or swing, rocking out to your favorite band, or gently swaying to some smooth jazz, dancing is an opportunity for a playful, sexually stimulating experience with your partner.

Remember When

Remember when you first discovered how thrilling lovemaking was with your partner, that initial tingle of excitement and butterflies-in-your-stomach feeling? Remember burning with sexual anticipation until you could get together again and rip each other's clothes off? Sex with your partner in the early days of your relationship may have been when it was the most playful and exciting. But that same heart-pounding, playful passion can be yours all over again when you remember that playful, burning-with-desire feeling you once had, and when you remember some of the things you used to do together to make it so.

Take a moment to recall the fun and excitement you had, and let yourself know all of that is waiting for you at home in the familiar, but still sexy, form of your loving partner. For example, let's say you and your partner had a fantastic romantic and sexual experience on your most recent New Year's Eve, or other special occasion. Everything about the evening played out like a beautiful dream. Your kids spent the night at your parents' house, so you had the place to yourselves. (How often does that happen?) You put on some soft, sexy music that reminds you both of the first time you slow danced. You prepared a delicious, sensual meal together, using the sexiest foods you could think of, food you could feed to each other like shrimp cocktail, strawberries dipped in chocolate, juicy slices of orange. You toasted to the love you share and to each other's health and happiness with the most delicious champagne you have ever tasted.

You both deeply breathed in the delicious aromas of the food and made a point of paying close attention to the dramatic mix of colors, aromas and tastes. The two of you started to kiss and slow dance in the middle of the kitchen before moving upstairs to the bedroom, where the two of you made love with absolutely zero worries about being interrupted or overheard. And afterward, as you laid in each other's arms, smiling and basking in the afterglow of your lovemaking, you told each other how relaxed, peaceful and content you felt.

Much like good wine, positive memories of romantic sexual encounters with your partner can actually grow richer, more satisfying, and more sexually stimulating with the passage of time. When people remember exciting past sexual encounters, they can also embellish them here and there with carefully chosen sexy details. That is to say, they can mix memory and fantasy together, and this potent combination can take them to a very hot, sexy, desire-filled place in their minds.

Many therapists and sex experts like to remind us that our minds are actually our most important sexual organ, since so much of what we find sexually desirable and enjoyable is rooted in our thoughts, senses, memories, fantasies, and (as we will discuss in the next section), in our feelings of excitement and anticipation about future sexual encounters with our partners. In other words, satisfying sex is as much a mental experience as it is an emotional and physical one. This means that it's useful to keep revisiting our most positive sexual memories and to incorporate these good memories into our fantasy lives to make our sex lives with our partners as exciting as possible. You may choose to share some of your sexiest recollections with your partner, who will probably enjoy strolling down sex memory lane just as much as you do, if not more so.

Many of the sexual memories we are most likely to call upon to boost our level of sexual desire tend to fall into one of three categories: (1) supercharged hot and erotic memories, (2) deeply intimate and romantic memories, and (3) a combination of the two.

Memories that fall into the last category in the sense that they blend romance and emotional intimacy with supercharged eroticism (such as the New Year's Eve memory described above), can actually be doubly useful when people recall them to trigger sexual desire. Of course, the more erotic portion of such memories is stimulating for obvious reasons. But for some people (and women in particular), one of the surest ways to boost sexual desire is to allow their minds to drift back to the most romantic and emotionally intimate times they have shared with their partners, rather than the most sexually erotic times.

Along these lines, keep in mind that it is not only your positive sexual memories that can turn you on before and/or during sexual encounters with your partner. Indeed, any positive memory—even positive memories that are not overtly sexual in nature—can serve as sexual stimulants. After all, human sexuality in general, and human sexual desire in particular, are highly subjective in nature. And some of the things that turn you on sexually may actually have very little (or even nothing) to do with sexual activity itself.

For instance, you may feel sexually turned on by intelligence and interesting conversation. For example, say you and your partner attended a lecture a few months ago at a local college, and afterward you had a lively debate about what you heard, and you enjoy thinking about that particular discussion to this day. Not only do you enjoy thinking about it because it makes you feel intellectually stimulated, but you also feel tingly and sexually alive at the recollection. This is a classic illustration of how a memory of a positive (yet not overtly sexual) experience can end up functioning as a sexual turn-on because of what that person happens to find sexy.

One final key point to consider regarding the ongoing interplay of memory and sex: The more positive sexual and nonsexual memories that you have stored up in your mental memory bank and in your body's memory, the more you will be able to boost your sexual desire and your capacity for enjoying sex. This can be particularly important if you also have some negative sexual memories lurking around in the back of your mind. The positive sexual memories that people have can be used as mental ammunition to combat any sexual inhibitions that may have developed in the aftermath of one or more unpleasant sexual experiences from the past.

This isn't to say that a person's good sexual memories can totally wipe the slate clean, especially if that individual has many negative sexual memories, and/or if those negative memories are not just unpleasant, dull or slightly embarrassing, but are actually traumatic in nature. Negative memories of past sexual experiences, and particularly traumatic sexual memories, can't simply be erased from a person's mind.

But it can be helpful for people who have been hurt or disappointed (rather than traumatized) by past sexual relationships to keep their minds and hearts open to the possibility that, *with the right partner*, sex can be extremely enjoyable and fulfilling. While each pleasurable sexual encounter may not help people totally erase their more unpleasant sexual memories, the positive memories they are now creating with their loving partners can help them counterbalance or offset the less pleasant ones.

In addition, everything people do to augment their arsenal of positive sexual experiences and memories can help them develop or increase what mental health experts call *emotional resilience*. Emotional resilience (also known as "emotional hardiness") can be an enormously powerful tool for coping with difficulties that arise in all areas of life, including sexual problems, such as a low level of desire.

def•i•ni•tion

Emotional resilience is the ability to bounce back following stressful experiences and not become emotionally trapped by difficult and/or emotionally painful situations. Emotionally resilient people mobilize all of their emotional inner resources to move beyond their stressful experiences as smoothly and as quickly as possible.

In Chapter 6, we provide a series of empirically based practical steps people can take to build up their reserves of emotional resilience, as well as their desire for sex. In Appendix B, we discuss in-depth how negative sexual memories can dampen people's feelings of sexual desire and/or cause them to feel sexually inhibited, even with loving partners.

Anticipation and Sex

Much in the same way that positive sexual memories can enhance your level of sexual desire, the anticipation of making love with your partner can also help get you in the mood. When you and your partner make a conscious choice to view sex as play time for grown ups, you may start to find yourselves looking forward to your lovemaking more and more during the day. You may even find yourself daydreaming about it at the most unexpected times. By deliberately choosing to view sex as play, you may start to think about—and crave—sex more than you have in quite some time. If you are not currently in the habit of thinking about and anticipating lovemaking with your partner, it's never too late to start!

For instance, the next time you are in the shower getting ready for your day, rather than running through your to do list in your mind, think about how wonderful it's going to feel to make love to your partner later that night. Isn't that a lot more fun than thinking about chores? Allow yourself to fully envision the scene. Think about the kissing and caressing, about how much good sex relaxes you after a tense day. Recall how intimate and tingly it feels to be skin-to-skin with your lover. After a long, stressful day, sex is one of the best gifts you give to each other. It is also one of the best gifts you can give to yourself.

You can also help increase each other's anticipation for sex. For instance, if the two of you know that you want to make love later that evening, you can give each other sexy little phone calls during the day, just to hint at what you'd like to do together once you get home. This is a simple—yet highly effective—way to get both of your motors running long before the main event, making the sex all the more exciting and satisfying when it actually takes place.

> **Notable Quotable**
>
> "When our bodies are joyous, our emotions are positive and our spirits are uplifted. Therefore, the gift of your beloved's body, more than anything else, can make you feel loved."
>
> —Daphne Rose Kingma, author of *True Love: How to Make Your Relationship Sweeter, Deeper, and More Passionate*

Reward Yourselves

Many people like to think of sex as the frosting on the cake of a busy day. And it most certainly can be, if you let it. After you race around all day long, working, doing errands, chauffeuring your kids here and there, sex is a wonderful gift and reward you and your partner can give to each other.

Think of sex as a much-deserved reward for being productive, achieving a goal, or even for just for making it through a tough day, and you will enhance your sexual desire and add sparks to your lovemaking.

One brief but important caveat to keep in mind when thinking about sex as a "reward" is that it's not healthy or kind to use sex as a reward in the controlling sense. That is, don't hold sex out as a tantalizing possibility, a potential reward for your partner's good behavior, only to later abruptly withdraw the offer if some minor mistake he makes ends up disappointing you in some way. Such punitive behavior can move the sexual part of your relationship into dangerous territory, because it involves using sex as a weapon.

Do you recall the 1980s Eddie Murphy stand-up comedy routine in which a kid, played by Murphy, pretends to tauntingly wave a delicious ice cream treat in another kid's face, only to pull it back and shout, "Psych!"? Well, it's never a good idea to play a cruel game of "Psych!" with your partner, especially when it comes to sex. Not only is it a particularly nasty and immature way to tease the one you love, but people who play these kinds of games may be setting up a decidedly unhealthy tone and precedent for future sexual interactions with their partners.

Sexual Stress Relief

Genuine physical benefits come from having enjoyable, satisfying sex with your partner on a regular basis. Stress reduction is definitely one such benefit. Of course, there is the most obvious stress-relieving function that sex serves: reaching orgasm and experiencing the deeply relaxed feeling that follows.

During a typical orgasm, many of the large muscle groups throughout your entire body (particularly in your abdominal and pelvic regions) constrict or tighten up and then relax in a way that can release an enormous amount of pent-up stress and tension.

However, achieving orgasm, and that lovely, relaxed post-coital feeling of satisfaction, is not the only stress-relieving aspect of having sex. Far from it! All of the affectionate, stimulating touch activity you have with your partner has a proven and powerful "anti-stress" effect on your body, your mind, and your spirit.

It's important to remember that stress isn't always all bad; there are positive stressors in life, too, like getting married, finding out you are pregnant, or getting a job promotion. These life transitions and many others do cause stress and trepidation in a relationship; after all, change—even *good* change—is always a complex emotional experience. Sex provides a tremendous relief outlet for even these positive stressors on life. We all need these complex life stressors because they make us feel truly alive and fulfilled. In fact, if you didn't have at least some stress in your life, you might end up feeling stagnant, unproductive, and unfulfilled. The important thing to remember is that sex plays a key role in relieving all types of stress.

An Emotional Release

Maybe you have shed tears or have felt utterly emotionally exhausted following a particularly intense lovemaking session, not because you were sad, but because you felt so deeply moved by the experience. You were likely experiencing an emotional catharsis, the sudden purging or relieving of emotional tensions, and some sexual encounters can certainly trigger this type of emotional experience.

def•i•ni•tion

An **emotional catharsis** involves the purging or releasing of certain tensions or unpleasant feelings. Crying, for instance, can provide an emotional catharsis triggered by certain situations. But in other contexts, sex can be the trigger for an emotional catharsis. People usually feel a profound sense of relief after experiencing an emotional catharsis, because they have successfully rid themselves of their stress and tension.

"Having a good cry" is a particularly dramatic example illustrating the sometimes emotionally cathartic nature of sex. But weeping is not the only way people experience an emotional catharsis following sex with their partners. Apart from crying, laughter and/or intimate, soul-baring conversations are two other ways that people can experience an emotional catharsis following sex.

One of the best parts of an emotional catharsis—whether it is sexually induced or not—is its function as a profound stress reliever.

Setting the Stage

Some couples make a tradition of adding a stress-relief component to their lovemaking through creating an environment that is both relaxing and romantic. They may, for instance, play soft music, dim the lights, and light scented candles. They may also opt to incorporate sensual and calming massage and aromatic massage oils into their lovemaking. Any combination of these special little touches can increase your desire for sex and make your sexual experiences with your partner all the more satisfying and stress relieving.

Let's Touch

Taking your time with kissing, cuddling, touching, and foreplay is another stress-relieving component of sex. When you slowly run your fingers (or a soft feather, or your tongue) along each other's arms, legs, neck, etc., any stress you may feeling melts away. You are getting yourselves into a state of relaxed readiness, meaning you are both putting yourselves into an emotional and physical state that is simultaneously calm and geared up for making love.

Also, massage (of all kinds, not just sensual) can be effective for reducing overall stress. In addition to bringing the two of you closer together and enhancing your physical and emotional bond, massage can release pent-up tension you may not have been aware of.

We all feel better, less stressed, and more in touch with our bodies when we are receiving loving tactile attention from our partners. Touch of all kinds—ranging from a 30-second shoulder rub, all the way up to a marathon lovemaking session—can relieve both physical and emotional stress and improve your overall health. While you are touching and massaging each other, be sure to enhance the experience with nurturing and sensual conversation.

Energy and Hormones

When the two of you make love, you'll be happy to hear that you are engaging in a strenuous form of exercise. Like all other forms of aerobic exercise, sex ramps up your heart rate, while simultaneously burning fat and calories. Hurray! One more fantastic reason to have even more great sex with your partner!

An important thing sex does is increase the level of endorphins and testosterone (the hormone of sexual desire) your body produces during aerobic exercise. When your body manufactures more endorphins, you can experience that wonderful, all-natural "runner's high" feeling that's so exhilarating and euphoric … even if the two of you haven't set foot outside of your bedroom!

What exactly are endorphins, and why do you feel so good when your body releases them? They are neurotransmitters manufactured by the brain to reduce pain and induce a feeling of euphoria (kind of like a natural form of morphine). In addition to exercising and having sex (and particularly achieving orgasm), some other natural ways to trigger your brain to release endorphins include positive thinking (thinking happy thoughts), feeling emotionally moved (by, say, reading a wonderful book or beholding a beautiful piece of art), eating chocolate (seriously, but there's no need to eat too much of it, since a couple bites will do the trick), and finally, bursting out in a huge fit of laughter (which, of course, fits in very nicely with our overall sex as play theme in this chapter).

Also, as with all forms of aerobic exercise, the more regularly you do it, the better you can manage your production of the hormone cortisol. This is so important, because too much cortisol is a sign of too much stress and can cause health problems that interfere with your sex life.

Love Booster

Since sex triggers the release of endorphins, and endorphins are known to make you feel not just happy but euphoric, that's all the more reason to have even more sex with your partner. So what are you waiting for? Go for it!

Cortisol is the stress hormone released by your adrenal glands when you feel under pressure and go into fight-or-flight mode.

def•i•ni•tion

Cortisol is the "fight-or-flight" hormone your body releases when you are under stress. Among other things, too much cortisol can raise blood pressure, impair thinking and thyroid function and cause hyperglycemia. Luckily, every time you have sex with your partner, not only are you relieving stress, and releasing feel-good endorphins, but as an added bonus, you are also reducing your body's overall **cortisol level**.

While this hormone gives you that quick burst of energy you need in particular situations, if you produce too much cortisol on a regular (or even chronic) basis, this can be damaging to your cognitive functioning, your thyroid health, and many other bodily functions. Too much cortisol can also lead to unwanted weight gain, particularly in the abdominal area. Sex helps you calm down and relax, and this can help keep cortisol at manageable levels, all the while stimulating the endorphins that give you energy and make you feel so good.

Your Connecting Point

Sex as stress relief helps you connect with your partner. Following up on the intimacy issues we explored in depth in Chapter 2, it's important to note that bonding—both sexually and emotionally—is not only great for the health of your relationship, but it is also an effective way to relieve stress. When the two of you feel connected, your stress level will lower, and your desire for sex will increase.

Just think about all these stress-reducing components together: the soft music, the dim lighting, the scented candles, the aromatic massage oils, your undiluted focus on each other, sensual touch and the feel-good hormones. Then, just to top it all off, add orgasms into the mix! When you consider lovemaking in this light, we think you will understand why it is such a valuable stress reliever for you and your partner.

> **Notable Quotable**
>
> Even the way you breathe during, before, and after sex can help to relieve stress. "Breathing can have a tremendous effect on sex. The more complete the breathing, the deeper the experience of sex. That's why some people say that relaxed and easy breathing is the gateway to sexual ease. In fact, breathing can by itself lead to ecstasy."
> —William Ashoka Ross, author of *The Wonderful Little Sex Book*

Nonsexual Stress Relief

Of course, sex is just one of ways that mature lovers relax and revel passionately in each other's company, but it's certainly not the only way. There are many forms of life-enhancing recreation couples can experience together that serve as healthy stress relievers and strengtheners of their emotional and sexual bond.

Simply put, the more relaxed you feel, the more you desire sex. And because relaxation enhances sexual desire, everything you do to feel more relaxed is bound to make you crave sex more. With that in mind, here are stress-reducing activities in addition to lovemaking you can incorporate into your daily life to help reduce stress and get your sexual juices flowing.

Walking

Taking long walks with your partner, a friend, or on your own can significantly ease tension and make you feel healthier. Whether you stroll around your neighborhood, in a park, or along the beach, walking is a great way to get fresh air. It's also an excellent, low-impact form of exercise that doesn't put too much pressure on your joints or muscles.

Deep Breathing

There are several different deep-breathing techniques to invoke calm, focus, and a sense of feeling "centered." One of the simplest, most straightforward methods involves inhaling slowly and deeply through your nose for a count of four or eight, depending on your preference, and then exhaling slowly out of your mouth (again for a count of four or eight).

Hobbies

If you have a favorite hobby, like gardening, dancing, or playing the guitar, try to keep your hobby an active part of your life in some capacity, even when your schedule gets busy. Having a creative outlet that you enjoy is one of the best ways to relieve stress and take care of yourself.

Treating Yourself

Every once in a while it can't hurt to treat yourself to a little pick-me-up gift. It doesn't have to be expensive or extravagant—some new lipstick from your local drug store will do the trick. It is, as they say, "the thought that counts." And in this case, the thought is: "I'm a good person and I deserve this little treat."

Escaping

If you love to read or watch movies, allow yourself to get lost in a novel or film as often as possible. Think of it as really inexpensive vacation time.

Some people prefer to read great literary works and watch serious, dramatic movies, whereas others like to read light, frothy books and watch movies that are similarly lighthearted. Choose books and movies that give you an "escape" and the ability to temporarily take a break out from your usual routine.

Vacations

If your budget and your schedule permit, take regular breaks and vacations. You don't need to spend a fortune or go away for weeks at a time, but it is helpful to get away sometimes. A weekend away can do wonders to get you out of the same old thing. It can be as easy as a road trip to a nearby big city or just holing up for a night or two at a romantic inn or spa right where you live.

And if at all possible, try not to bring work along, so that you feel like you are really getting away from it all, both mentally and physically.

Routines and Rituals

Some people have certain things they do every day that's important to them to keep balance and focus in their lives. These routines and rituals are a great preventative stress measures.

They can be anything from spending a few minutes each day sitting in your favorite chair with your feet up, sipping a little decaffeinated herbal tea, to writing in a journal, to reading the sports page every morning. Incorporating simple activities like this into your day gives you your very own personalized stress-management program.

Meditating and Visualization

Meditation is another effective stress reliever. You can use meditation time to focus on your breathing and to clear your mind completely. Or you might prefer visualization exercises, such as picturing yourself in a beautiful, relaxing setting like a beach or a meadow. Both of these techniques help promote a sense of calmness.

Try this visualization of yourself lying on the beach with your mate. The sky is cobalt blue, the water is crystal clear, and the sand is white and fine. You have the whole beach to yourselves and you have both just taken a refreshing dip in the ocean. Now the sun and the sand are warming your skin.

The water is still dripping from your bodies. He helps you towel off and starts complimenting you, telling you how beautiful you look and how wonderful your skin feels. You start kissing and cuddling. One thing leads to another, until the two of you are making love on your own private, luxurious beach.

Does that help you put aside your worries and unwind a little bit? Not to mention make you want to run home and make love? Remember, when you take some time to relax and de-stress your mind, your body, and your soul, you are setting the stage for some fantastic sex!

Source of Rejuvenation

If you are currently so busy or overwhelmed that you sometimes view sex as a chore or task to complete and cross it off your "to do" list, it's important to change your attitude as soon as possible. One way is to view sex as a source of rejuvenation, as an energizing force in your life. You will be amazed at how quickly the feeling of sex as a chore will become sex as a delight!

Sex doesn't only rejuvenate you from a physical standpoint, it replenishes your supply of emotional energy, too. Sex gives you that little extra bounce or spring in your step that can lift your spirits and help you face the challenges and demands of your day.

Love Booster

Any time you'd like a quick burst of energy and vitality, rather than reaching for a cup of coffee, consider reaching for your partner instead. It's much more fun *and* more satisfying. And unlike caffeinated beverages, having too much sex won't give you the jitters, it will actually relax you.

A Creative Outlet

Take the opportunity of lovemaking with your partner to express your creativity and break out of typical sex routines. Some couples share fantasies to act out when making love. They may even dress up in costumes to make their particular fantasy come to life. When two partners team up in this way, they are co-writing, co-directing, and, of course, co-starring in a sexy play for their shared pleasure and stimulation.

Women who are big fans of romance novels like to engage in this kind of role-playing with their partners. They may even like to act out certain arousing scenes from their favorite books. Remember, you can choose to share your sexual fantasies with your partner, or you can keep them to yourself and just think about them before and during sex as a highly effective means of enhancing your sexual desire. (We will continue this discussion about sexual fantasies in Chapter 4, which is all about physical turn-ons.)

Just as some couples like to engage in fantasy-sharing and role-playing as a way of expressing their sexual creativity and enhancing their sexual desire, others like to plan romantic getaways at hotels, beaches, bed and breakfasts, campgrounds, spas, or wherever they are most comfortable. Indeed, many people find that making love in a sexy, romantic new and different environment can work wonders for waking up their senses and injecting fresh creativity into their sex life.

And don't forget to pack your sexy lingerie! After all, you're not staying at a romantic getaway to work or use the gym. You are staying in this tantalizingly unfamiliar setting to make love to your partner as often and in as many creative, stimulating ways as possible.

Different people seek different goals in a romantic getaway. Perhaps the two of you feel most sexually creative and most profoundly in touch with your sensuality when you travel off the beaten path and are surrounded by nature. If this is the case, you may want to go hiking and camping in the wilderness rather than staying at a fancy hotel.

Or perhaps you both prefer a spa atmosphere where you can not only get reacquainted with each other in the bedroom but you can also treat yourselves to massages, indulge in mud baths or sea salt rubs, and just generally seek out relaxation together and peace of mind.

Remember the specific location doesn't matter. What matters is finding a new and different setting where you both feel comfortable enough to break out of your sexual routine in new, fresh and imaginative ways.

The Great Distracter

In the best sense of the term, sex is a great distraction. It's an ideal way to give yourself a little "time-out," and we don't mean the kind that's having to sit in the corner by yourself! When you are fully engaged— mind, body, and soul—in making love with your partner, all of your attention focuses on the wonderful physical sensations that you and your partner are experiencing as a couple. And, at least for the duration of your foreplay and your lovemaking, your cares and worries will feel miles away.

Sex with your partner also offers a unique, exciting, healthy distraction from your daily routine, so let yourself get diverted!

Everyone needs brief, healthy escapes from their workaday lives. So allow yourself to get lost in your lovemaking experience with your mate. We aren't suggesting that you use sex to check out of reality altogether, but certainly for a little while at least. Sex may be exactly what you and your partner both need to temporarily escape from whatever may be troubling, even boring you, outside of the bedroom.

Ultimate Solace

Sometimes having sex with your partner can be a source of comfort. If you have had a terrible day or are going through a difficult time, for instance, you may seek out your partner for some much-needed cuddling and emotional support. And sometimes that cuddling and support leads to making love. It might not be wildly acrobatic lovemaking, but more on the soft and gentle end of the spectrum to give you the closeness and comfort you need. Either way, the benefits sex can provide for feelings of comfort and solace are enormous, both emotionally and physically.

Spiritual Connections

Sex with your beloved can be viewed as a spiritual union of two souls, as two hearts becoming one, or as a means of connecting in some way with the Divine.

After all, love is at the center of many religious faiths (both the love that we feel for one another and the love that we feel for a Higher Power). And making love with your partner is, of course, the physical manifestation of that love the two of you share.

Moments of Transcendence

Many people believe that the key to having a more satisfying love life is to get in close touch with their spiritual side. They feel that it is no accident that it's possible to experience sublime "moments of transcendence" or ecstatic states both during lovemaking and during prayer.

Also, if you recall our discussion about "The Generous Gesture" in Chapter 2, you know that being a giver during sex is often more enjoyable than being a taker. Any time you give generously of yourself, you are conducting yourself in a spiritually enlightened way, even in the bedroom.

Time Out of Time

Theologians and other religious thinkers often use the expression "time out of time" to refer to any sacred or extraordinary time that feels different from mundane time. A spiritual ritual or celebration, for example, may feel like this due to its sacred nature. During such special moments, time can feel almost as if it is standing still.

For instance, graduating from high school and throwing your mortar boards up in the air with all of your classmates can feel like time out of time, or a magical time that feels somehow elevated above or at least separate from regular time.

Perhaps some of your favorite, most memorable sexual experiences with your partner have felt like this, when all the clocks seemed to slow down or stop, because you felt so close and so deeply connected to each other.

Any one of your romantic encounters with your partner has the potential to soar to such heights, not only in terms of physical ecstasy, but also in terms of emotional intimacy. You might not see stars every time the two of you have sex, but you certainly will have the chance to experience what feels like a truly transcendent moment with each new encounter.

The Here and Now

Tuning into the "here and now" is another potentially spiritual dimension of sex.

In other words, if you decide that for the duration of your lovemaking you are going to shut out the world, focus on the here and now, and zero in on your partner's touch and words, the overall experience will be more intense, exciting, and gratifying. Good sex can transport you to another place physically, emotionally, and psychologically. Of course, not every sexual experience is going to take you to the land of ecstasy, but some will, *especially* if you prepare yourself for that possibility by shutting everything else out and focusing all of your energy on the here and now of your lovemaking experience with your partner.

 Love Booster

When you have sex with your partner, pour every ounce of your attention and energy into your lovemaking. Give it your all, so that you can both get the most out of it.

A Self-Esteem Booster

In Chapter 6, we will explore in greater detail the complex relationship between sex and self-esteem. But for now, let's look specifically at one particular aspect of the relationship between sex and self-esteem: how feeling sexy and appealing enhances sexual desire.

Love Booster

When you feel good about yourself, both inside and out, it shows in your skin, your eyes, your posture, and even in the way you walk. Not only that, but all of this positive, feel-good energy also enhances your sexual desire.

A big part of feeling sexual desire is feeling attractive and sexually desirable, and part of feeling sexually desirable is taking the time to make yourself feel attractive. For instance, if styling your hair in a certain way, or wearing a certain shade of lipstick, has always given you a little shot of confidence, then be sure to do these things regularly. While there is no need to become obsessed with your physical appearance, it's not a good idea to ignore the way you look, either. Your physical appearance is certainly not everything, but it does matter, at least to a certain extent.

After all, when you take care of your appearance, you are sending the message to yourself, your partner and the rest of the world that you value yourself, and that you are worth the time and effort it takes to look put-together.

So even if the two of you have been together for years, when you take the time to look good, you are sending your partner two equally important messages: (1) I still like to look nice for you; and (2) I still like to look nice for me.

This does not mean that you have to slather on a ton of cosmetics, especially if that is not (and has never been) your style. Rather, it means that when you take care of yourself (both inside and out), it shows. You walk around with an inviting and sexy inner glow of someone who values herself and invests time and energy in her health and well-being. And what could be sexier than that?

Your Safe Haven

To one degree or another, we all go through times in our lives when our guards and defenses are up. It's only natural. Luckily, sex with your loving partner enables you to lower those defenses so you can have a more fully enjoyable experience. In other words, the bedroom you share with your lover is your safe haven from the rest of the world, one of the few places where you can just relax and feel totally comfortable, tranquil and at ease.

All the World's a Stage

In *As You Like It*, Shakespeare wrote: "All the world's a stage, and all the men and women merely players." Much like professional actors, we all tend to put on different faces for the different roles we are required to play during the course of our daily lives. This does not mean that we are phonies or fakes, only that different parts of our day require different facets of our personalities to rise to the forefront.

For example, if you are the manager of a business, you will have to act like the boss, like the person in charge, even when you don't particularly feel like playing this part. You will need to maintain a tone of authority that commands respect in the way you speak and carry yourself.

Or maybe you are an early-childhood teacher. You spend your days using your imagination, reading stories, helping little hands with various tasks like painting, drawing, and cutting, and doling out gentle discipline as needed.

The point is that no matter what you do or how much you enjoy it (or not), your work life requires you to step into your designated role as teacher or manager, even parent; but remember you can step out of those roles once you get home and back into the arms of your loving partner, and especially into the bedroom.

Dropping Your Guard

As we said, home is your safe haven, and your bedroom, in particular, is your sacred sanctuary. This is where you can cast all of your outside-world roles aside and slip into the best role of all: your naked, authentic self.

We're not talking only about being naked physically (although we are, of course, talking about that). We're also referring to emotional nakedness or the ability to "let it all hang out" (emotionally speaking) with your partner, both during lovemaking and in general.

Simply put, having sex with your loving partner is the one time you can drop any and all pretenses. And what could be more stress-relieving and enjoyable than being your authentic self with your loving, accepting partner?

No Need to Be Shy

On a slightly different (but still related) topic, people who consider themselves shy often have one person with whom they feel truly comfortable. And for many shy people, that one person tends to be their partner.

So if you consider yourself or your partner on the shy or self-conscious side around most people, you probably know that having sex can provide you and your partner with a highly effective way to drop the usual inhibitions and feelings of shyness.

The Power of Love

One of the biggest advantages of being married to (or deeply committed to) your true love is being accepted for who you are. You can drop your guard completely and you will never be hurt.

A loving partner will always want to build you up and nourish your mind, body, and soul. When you take the time to think about his many wonderful qualities, all the many reasons you fell madly in love with him in the first place, and all the ways he loves you just for you, you may very well find that your sexual desire for your mate goes through the roof.

The Least You Need to Know

- Sex is a way committed lovers can play together and have fun with their intimate bond as a couple.

- Maintain a positive, playful, lighthearted attitude toward your sex life. When people overanalyze sex, or take it too seriously, they inadvertently suck most of the fun and joy right out of it.

- Sex is a great stress reliever and energy booster. It produces endorphins and other feel-good hormones and gives you physical and emotional energy.

- For many people, making love with their partners includes a strong spiritual component and makes them feel more connected with the sacred aspects of life.

Part 2

Getting In Touch with Your Sensuality

Sexual desire and arousal are deeply personal experiences, and what drives one person wild with passion may do absolutely nothing for another (and vice versa). Also, how you feel about yourself translates into how you feel, act, and respond in the bedroom.

This part will familiarize you with the physical and emotional dimensions of sexual desire and arousal, and help you figure out what makes you and your partner feel sexy, turned on, and connected.

I THOUGHT WE'D TRY SOMETHING NEW TONIGHT.

Chapter 4

Physical Turn-Ons

In This Chapter

- Openly showing your affection enhances your mutual sexual desire
- Erotic scenarios, reading materials, and mainstream movies can work wonders for your sex life
- Hot sex is possible for those who have been married or together for a long time
- Seduction is an exciting and erotic gift
- Key learnings from research on sexual desire

Let's now explore a wide range of physically stimulating activities that can enhance your sexual desire for your partner. Sexual desire and sexual arousal are rooted in certain key physical activities, ranging from rubbing, kissing, touching, and massaging, all the way up to sexual intercourse. Think of your sex life (and your communication about your sex life) in terms of an erotic flow, imagining your own pleasure and your partner's pleasure as a wave that is continually flowing back and forth between the two of you.

Rediscovering Your Sexuality Together

A strong sexual bond requires couples to commit to this exciting process of mutual discovery, and to talk about what they most enjoy in bed as well as what they might like to try in the future. In addition to talking, however, couples also need to keep at it on a regular basis. In other words, talking about sex is instructive (and a lot of fun, too), but at the same time, couples need to continue having sex, not just discussing it. In this way, they can continually refine the steps and techniques that suit their respective and mutual tastes.

You will find that if you and your partner make a consistent effort to make love regularly, and to communicate about what turns you both on, you will both reap big rewards! It can be a lot of fun to talk with your partner about what turns you both on physically. For instance, you may talk about how exciting it would be to kiss more or to kiss differently, both in general and during sex. Or you might want to create erotic scenarios, both privately (i.e., in your own minds), and together, as an intimate, erotic team of two acting out your wildest fantasies. Or you may find yourselves getting all hot and bothered during a detailed conversation about what kinds of foreplay work best for both of you. You get the picture.

Always bear in mind that there is no one right way to be sexual. Happy, rewarding sex is what you both decide works well for the two of you. You may want to think of this concept as sexual teamwork (an idea we will explore further in the final chapter.)

Don't buy into the negative spin on sex that's out there about partners who have been married or together for a long time. Some nay-sayers make the argument that while your love for and commitment to each other remains a constant force in your life, your lust for each other is bound to decline over time. Don't pay any attention to that, because there is a much different approach and exciting reality to this important subject. Understandably your sex life changes after the honeymoon phase comes to an end. But your desire for one another is always there; it's percolating just under the surface of your busy lives, and it's just waiting to be acknowledged, tapped into, and thoroughly enjoyed!

Of course, keeping the sex going and the passion alive in a relationship doesn't just happen magically. If your current sex life is not as hot and happening as you'd like it to be, the two of you will need to get a little creative. But we promise it will be exciting! (Like a walk on the wild side, creative sex can be truly exhilarating.) This chapter contains tips and strategies in a physical sense to reawaken your desire and put that extra zing back into your sex life.

Public and Private Displays of Affection

We have all known couples who engage in public displays of affection. They're the ones who are always all over each other like a pair of teenagers in love. For example, perhaps they give each other little kisses or back rubs, or even light slaps on the bottom whenever they pass each other in the hallway. Maybe they have been together 5 or 10 or 15 years or longer. Sometimes their displays get to the point their friends tease them and say, "Get a room already."

Well, instead of telling the couple to get a room, maybe these friends should be offering them some heart-felt congratulations. Clearly this affectionate couple is onto something. They understand that being close and affectionate with each other can happen at any time and place, including in public. Whether they realize it or not, they are seizing every opportunity to get closer to their partner, physically and emotionally, and this can fuel the fires of passion in the bedroom.

On the other hand, maybe public displays of affection aren't for you and your partner. Perhaps the two of you have always had a sort of unspoken hands-off policy in the presence of other people. That's perfectly fine, too. Showing affection in public isn't for everyone.

Even if that's the case, however, in the privacy of your own home, be sure to engage in private displays of affection as frequently as possible, because loving, flirtatious gestures help fan the flames of sexual desire.

Of course private displays of affection are just that: private. This means they can range from the same light kissing, hand-holding and back rubbing that some couples feel comfortable doing in public all the way up to deep kissing and, naturally, making love.

Tantalizing Talk

You and your partner may find yourselves firmly entrenched in the endless parade of demands and obligations that come with leaving young adulthood behind and becoming full-fledged grown-ups. But before the two of you became parents, property owners, and mortgage holders, you were lovers first. Sure, you were (and still are) best friends, too. But back in the day, the two of you were on fire!

To recapture that sizzling passion from your honeymoon phase, set aside some days or nights that are all about the two of you and no one else. Remember, this is about teamwork and exploring your sexual needs and desires *together*. So the first step is to open up! Talk about your feelings, and especially your fantasies, even if talking about them makes you blush a bit at first. For instance, if there is a position or technique that you've always dreamed of trying but have been too shy to discuss, take a deep breath and share this thought with your partner. Your partner will more than likely be thrilled that you decided to share your fantasy with her. And chances are she will want to try it, too. It doesn't get any more win-win than that!

Sometimes long-term partners make the (often-faulty) assumption that they have already explored all of their sexual frontiers together, that there is nothing left to try. Or perhaps it's been quite a while since they attempted a particular technique they once greatly enjoyed, and they wonder if it's worth trying again. That's why simply talking with your partner about your past, present, and possible future turn-ons can be such a turn-on!

Deep Talk Versus Hot Sex

As you know, we are advocates of emotional intimacy, and the more connected the two of you feel as friends and confidants, the more physical desire you will feel for each other.

However, not all couples like to mix intimate, soul-baring conversations in with sex, and this is understandable. But on the other hand, some do.

When you share something deep and meaningful, you often feel raw, vulnerable, and exposed, even with your beloved, trusted partner. Often what you want and need afterward is cuddling and protection, not hot sex. Yet others, on the other hand, may prefer to go right into having sex, as that may be an extension of the conversation in a way they want to have it. Either way, you and your partner should decide what's right for the both of you in each deep-talk circumstance you have.

The Sorbet Rule

Picture a fancy meal being served at a high-end restaurant. Between courses, the waiter may serve the diners a sorbet, and he does this for a couple of reasons. First, he wants the diners to have moment to digest and savor the previous course. And second, he wants to help them cleanse their palates before the next course, which offers a totally different (but equally satisfying) taste sensation from the previous one.

def•i•ni•tion

The **Sorbet Rule** refers to the idea that many couples like to have a little buffer activity between their soul-baring conversations (emotional intimacy) and their lovemaking (physical intimacy). For many couples, kissing functions as their favorite sorbet. For example, a deep conversation could be followed by slow, gentle kissing that gradually grows more passionate until it turns into lovemaking.

This sorbet metaphor is handy when you think about creative ways to foster the healthy co-existence of emotional intimacy and passionate sex in your relationship. You and your partner certainly need both if you want your relationship to stay happy, strong, and on course; so you may also need a little sorbet or a buffer zone to transition from sharing confidences to making love.

There are simple, physically tantalizing ways to make this transition smooth and seamless. To ease out of deep-talk mode into sex, even hot-sex mode, all that's required is some kissing. With this kind of transitional kissing, where you are switching gears from confiding and emotional-intimacy mode to lovemaking and physical-intimacy mode, it's good to start out slowly and gently, and gradually build into a more passionate making out session. Once you are in full-blown making-out mode, it feels natural and right to start making love.

Love Booster _____

After a deep, emotionally satisfying conversation with your partner, let him know it's finally time to get down to business by changing into a sexy outfit and kissing him seductively.

Perhaps a slinky red camisole serves as your lovemaking signal to your mate. When you slip it on, or when he says he would like you to slip it on, this exchange serves as your palate-cleansing sorbet, or means of transitioning out of talking mode and into sex mode.

Of course there are exceptions to every rule, the sorbet rule included. One specific type of sharing is a great lead-in to sex (no palate-cleansing "sorbet" needed!). As we mentioned at the beginning of this chapter, the confiding of sexual fantasies is one kind of deep, secret-baring talk that can definitely lead straight into passionate lovemaking!

Getting In The Mood for Love

Even if you've had a long or aggravating day, helping to get each other in the mood for love can be physically arousing. Some examples might include preparing a nice meal for your partner, or preparing dinner together, sharing a glass of wine, or taking a sensual shower or bath together. And why wait for Valentine's Day to sprinkle rose petals on the comforter, or to buy your partner a dozen red roses, or even just one? By simply starting to engage in sexual behavior, kissing, and intimate touching, you can both get in the mood for love.

In a recent interview we conducted via e-mail with Patty Brisden, the founder of www.pureromance.com, she had this advice for people looking for exciting new physical turn-ons to enhance their sexual desire: "Think outside the box (box springs, that is): we all know the bedroom is a couple's safe haven, but that doesn't mean all of your romantic interludes need to begin and end there. Why not lay out a soft blanket in the living room? Light candles and celebrate your relationship with a bottle of Champagne and strawberries."

Love Booster _____

Rather than thinking, I'm too tired and drained to have sex tonight, think: I'm so tired; sex is exactly what I need right now to feel better!

Brisden maintains that, "After years of being intimate, many couples become almost robotic in their attempts at foreplay and intimacy." She believes that thinking outside the box "is a great way to get you both touching and massaging each other with affection and desire."

Dressing the Part

Sexy lingerie is a popular, great technique to get you and your partner in the mood. This is something you can do both for yourself and for your partner. He will, of course, love the sight of you in something sexy. Men respond strongly to visual sexual cues.

Remember, lingerie comes in all colors, styles, patterns, shapes and sizes, and it's not only intended for six-foot tall fashion models. And these days, there is so much to choose from! Every mall across the U.S. contains at least one store that specializes in selling intimate apparel. And if you prefer to shop from home for sexy attire, you can do so with print catalogues or go online. In fact, if you type the words "lingerie" and "retailers" into any search engine, many fantastic and varied listings will come up. And one or more of these retailers are bound to have several items that suit your taste and body shape.

But more than this, you will feel sexy, too. There is nothing quite like silk or satin, the way it clings to your curves, making you feel womanly and desirable. And of course, feeling desirable is a potent aphrodisiac, because people who feel sexy and appealing to their partners tend to feel more sexual desire as well.

Sexy Mainstream Movies

It likely comes as no surprise to learn that watching sexy movies with your partner can be a tremendous physical turn-on. In fact, there are many R-rated mainstream films with scenes that are hot and sexy without being obscene or offensive.

Some sexy mainstream films (with plots ranging from interesting to downright compelling) include the following:

- *The Unbearable Lightness of Being*, starring Lena Olin, Daniel Day Lewis, and Juliette Binoche

Love Booster _____

Just because you start watching a sexy movie together doesn't mean you have to finish watching it! If what you're watching makes you both feel hot and bothered, don't hold back. Act on your impulse to make love then and there.

♦ *9 ½ Weeks*, with Kim Basinger and Mickey Rourke

♦ *Out of Sight*, with George Clooney and Jennifer Lopez

♦ *The Grifters*, starring Annette Bening and John Cusack

♦ *Risky Business*, starring Tom Cruise and Rebecca DeMornay

♦ *Original Sin*, with Angelina Jolie and Antonio Banderas

♦ *Bull Durham*, starring Susan Sarandon, Kevin Costner, and Tim Robinson

♦ *Unfaithful*, starring Diane Lane, Oliver Martinez, and Richard Gere

All of these movies feature at least one or two hot and naughty (but not overly explicit) sex scenes that can be highly effective for enhancing sexual desire, particularly when you watch them together.

Erotic Reading Material

Some couples read erotic literature out loud to each other to turn one another on. If this interests you, one sexually charged writer whose work you may enjoy is Anaïs Nin, who wrote *Delta of Venus* and *Henry and June*. (You may recall this second classic of erotic literature inspired a film by the same name starring Uma Thurman, Fred Ward, and Maria de Medeiros.) Many people (and especially women) who read her work feel that even though she wrote her erotic books several decades ago, she really got it. That is, she had a keen and nuanced understanding of what really turns people on, women in particular.

You and your partner may also want to read erotic story collections written specifically for couples to enjoy together. For instance, *The Erotic Edge: 22 Erotic Stories For Couples*, edited by Lonnie Barbach, is a collection of sexy stories that features the work of both male and female writers of erotica.

Men and women often find different types of erotic literature appealing. To acknowledge this fact, entire new fields of erotic literature (sometimes known as herotica or romantica) have been springing up to cater to the individual erotic tastes of women and couples.

Pornography

No book about sex and couples would be complete without some mention of pornography. Pornography has been around for ages, but has become a bigger factor in many people's lives and relationships since the dawning of the Internet era.

Some couples enjoy watching hardcore pornographic movies or looking at pornographic magazines together and feel that it strongly enhances their sex lives. Nonetheless, for many couples, hardcore pornography (particularly online pornography) has become a point of contention in their relationship.

If you're concerned that online porn may be interfering in any way with your relationship with your partner, here are beginning steps to get the conversation started toward resolution:

- Say to your partner: "I enjoy our lovemaking and want both of us to enjoy good sex."

- Ask your partner: Is there something we could do together to make our sexual relationship better?"

- Let your partner know: "I am concerned that online pornography is getting in our way."

- Reassure your partner: "I want us to be closer and I am willing to figure this out together."

Overall, our main message about pornography is that it's up to you and your partner to determine *together* what role you would like it to play in your relationship, if any. If one of you feels hurt or damaged in any way by its usage, speak up! And if pornography continues to be a problem even after the two of you have talked about it, please consider discussing the issue with a couples therapist. That way you can work collaboratively, and with the assistance of a trained professional, on finding solutions that are genuinely satisfactory to both of you. After all, as we have been saying all along, communication (even, perhaps especially, about topics that you find difficult or upsetting), is one of the biggest keys to keeping all aspects of your relationship (including your sex life) on track.

Hot Sex For Committed Couples

As we mentioned earlier, people often assume that it's the "wild, swinging singles" who are having all the fun, sexually speaking. But this is not always the case. Married people and long-time partners can and do have sex lives that are just as hot and passionate as their single peers. The commonly held belief that married sex is pleasant, mild, and lacking in passion paints a one-dimensional picture of lovemaking between committed individuals. And in many cases, it is just plain wrong. Indeed, hot sex among long-term couples is not only achievable, but it is happening as we speak, and it can be happening to you.

There will always be sit-coms, movies, and books that make fun of married life and try to equate getting married with the end of good times. But for many people, marriage, or commitment, is when the true fun begins! After all, you married or fully committed to each other because you felt close to begin with, and you knew that you wanted to grow even closer.

Your sexual relationship will always be an essential part of your connection and commitment to each other, so why not make it the most it can be. In a committed relationship, you experience a sense of intimacy that can't compare to any of your previous relationships. You no longer need to be self-conscious and you can truly be yourself. This feeling of liberation is itself a big turn-on you can translate into hot sex with your beloved.

When you mix things up by sharing a fantasy or performing a sexy striptease or lap dance, or trying something else totally new in bed, it's not just for the sake of trying something different—it's also to strengthen your love and to take your feelings of intimacy, connectedness and commitment to an even higher level.

We All Contain Multitudes

An effective way to mix things up and keep your monogamous sex life fresh and exciting is to observe and pay close attention to the mysteries that lie within the familiar.

In his celebrated poem, "Song of Myself," Walt Whitman wrote, "I contain multitudes." It's true that we *all* contain multitudes, and yet it's something we often forget about both ourselves and our partners. Have you ever noticed that when you see your partner in a different context or in a different light, you often feel an erotic charge, a burst of sexual desire?

For instance, what if, one day, your husband, who usually dresses casually for work has to get dressed up for a special meeting. The sexy combination of how handsome he looks in a suit, the knowing expression on his face, the confidence in his voice and the way he carries himself can make you want him sexually.

Or maybe you feel turned on by the fact that he runs five miles a day, or that he has an amazing singing voice. Like all of us, your partner has a million sides or layers to his personality, some of which you already know, and some of which you'll continue to discover over the course of time. And part of being in love with (and sexually desiring of) each other now and in the future has to do with gradually unearthing (like a pair of love archaeologists) these fascinating layers of personality that lie within each of you.

What exactly is transpiring when you see your partner in a different light and it turns you on? It's just your good old familiar hubby, right? The same guy who last night threw on his ripped sweatpants and a dirty t-shirt to take the garbage out to the curb?

Well, yes and no.

He both is and isn't the same guy. (Once again, remember those wise Walt Whitman's words.) Last night, when he was wearing his ancient, tattered sweatpants, he was in full-blown domestic/nesting mode. And when you saw him dressed like that, we're guessing that hot, no-holds-barred, down-and-dirty sex might not have been the first thing to cross your mind. Oh, you might have thought other nice things about him, like "He's such a cutie-pie," or "I'm so lucky that he's so sweet and helpful around the house." But you might not have been thinking that you want to tear his comfy old clothes off and ravage him right on the spot ... which is precisely what you *were* thinking when you saw him all dressed up in his snazzy suit, or running, or singing and playing guitar.

When two people are in a marriage or long-term, committed relationship, it's true they become much less mysterious and far more familiar to each other over the course of time. And we certainly don't have to be reminded of that nasty old cliché "familiarity breeds contempt."

But this is precisely where the notion that each of us contains multitudes comes in handy, because it means that even in the most familiar, domesticated, comfy and cozy of committed relationships, a sexy spark of the mysterious and the unknown remains burning.

To put it simply, as well as the two of you know each other—and if you're reading this book, we're guessing the two of you probably know each other pretty darn well by now—you both still have the capacity to surprise each other, because no one person can ever know another person completely. Heck, we don't even know ourselves completely. Since we are all growing and learning and changing constantly, we are not exactly the same people we were five years ago, or even one year ago.

You may find this idea that no one can ever fully know anyone else vaguely frightening or upsetting at first. But it's really exciting when you think about it, particularly where sexual desire is concerned. After all, if your partner still has the capacity to surprise you by revealing different facets of himself every now and then—and often at the most unexpected times—this means that your story as a couple is still unfolding. And very likely there are plenty more interesting surprises to come!

Also, if your partner still has the capacity to surprise you, well then, you still have the capacity to surprise him, too. Every new day that you spend together offers you an opportunity to do or say the unexpected, to seduce him in a fresh and innovative way. And doing—or wearing, or saying—the unexpected can keep things hot and passionate in the bedroom. For instance, just because up until now you may never have greeted him at the door wearing nothing but high heels, that doesn't mean you might not do just that tomorrow!

Looking at your partner in a different light or from a different angle offers you a glimpse of the multitudes that lie within him. Likewise, looking at yourself in a different light or from a different angle can give you some insight into the various facets of your own self. This means that it's not only your partner who has the capacity to surprise you (in bed or in any other department). You also have the capacity to surprise yourself, and to tap into your feelings of sexual desire in brand new, previously unexplored ways.

Naughty and Nice

Some couples often agree to be nice and respectable people out in public, but let themselves be naughty when they are together in the privacy of their own bedroom. This becomes their special secret and a deliciously risqué part of their bond. And this functions as a great physical turn-on when you know what's waiting for you when you get home.

Also, people who have been married or committed to each other for years share many inside jokes. They can turn what starts out as a lark into a great seduction scene. For instance, maybe the two of you share a mutual fantasy about being a couple of strangers who meet in a hotel and fall in lust at first glance. Well, why not take this fantasy to the next level by acting it out together?

At first, the whole scenario may make you both feel silly. It may even give you both a case of the giggles. And that's perfectly fine. Remember, sex is play time! And laughter is an important part of play time. But then, after you both get the laughter out of your systems, you may decide that the whole scenario of two "nice" strangers meeting and making mad, passionate "naughty" love in a hotel is actually pretty darn erotic after all, and you may both get into it with great gusto.

Other similar scenarios are the sexy delivery guy meets foxy, lonely housewife, the sexy nurse treats a hot, lonely patient, or any other erotic, mutually stimulating vignette you care to imagine and act out together.

A client we'll call Leesa talked about the pleasures of creating erotic scenarios with her partner. In Leesa's words, "There is no purpose to acting out our fantasies other than to have fun! I would pretend to be a courtesan and he would be an innocent young man with no sexual experience. I would set the scene with candlelight, incense, and nonalcoholic wine, as he doesn't drink. I would wear a mid-thigh red silk robe and black lace underpants with a tiny red heart on them. He would wear a white shirt and skinny tie and look like a nerd. He would hesitantly tap on the door; when I opened it, he would hand me a small bouquet of flowers. I took it from there!"

I asked Leesa, "How did you get over any embarrassment about creating scenes?"

Leesa responded, "Surprisingly, it wasn't embarrassing, and I didn't feel the least bit self-conscious. I'm not even sure why, because normally even the simplest acting is difficult for me. At women's gatherings, where we have to do spontaneous things like sing or dance, I am paralyzed. I'm actually very inhibited!

"But probably because the character Markus chose to play was naïve and nerdy, I felt a sense of power. And of course, wearing red silk and black lace underpants makes one fearless!"

So remember, just because you've been together a long time, and are a certain face in public, doesn't mean you don't have complete freedom to be naughty in private with your partner and create erotic scenarios to spice up your sex life.

The Art of Seduction

Some couples like to give each other "the eye" at parties, just as they used to do during their dating days. It's fun and exciting to flirt in public, not necessarily in an over-the-top way, but just in a way that lets you both know you'll be making love when you get home.

The myth that married and long-term couples lose the power to seduce their mates is just that: a myth. The fact is that these couples can be just as easily enticed by their partners into making love as newlyweds. In fact, sometimes when your partner is complaining about how much her day took out of her, she may be secretly hoping you will do everything in your sexual power to take her worries away by seducing her right on the spot!

Some people actually like the challenge of trying to seduce their partner when she claims to be beyond persuasion. Think about it: people love to be seduced. It makes them feel wanted and adored.

Your Partner's Pleasure Is Your Pleasure

Another physical turn-on for many people is watching their partner reach orgasm. This moment is enjoyable for the partner achieving orgasm, obviously, but it can be just as, and sometimes more, enjoyable for the other partner who's watching. Seeing your spouse or partner, the person you love most in the world, reach such glorious heights of physical and emotional ecstasy, with and because of your involvement, can be a tremendous turn-on.

Erogenous Zones

Couples who have been together for a long time know each other's favorite erogenous zones—the places that really turn them on—and positions (though perhaps not all of them; it never hurts to ask about more!) A man may know, for example, that if he kisses his partner on the back of her neck near her right ear that he can cause her to shudder with pleasure. And a woman may know that if she runs a light feather over her partner's chest, he will be so turned on that he will grab her and make love to her right that minute.

def•i•ni•tion

An **erogenous zone** is any sexually sensitive part of the body that is aroused when kissed, touched, rubbed or massaged. Different people have different erogenous zones, so it's important to become familiar with your partner's, and your own. Obvious erogenous zones are the genitals, breasts and buttocks, but other common ones include the tongue, lips, neck, shoulders, waist, hips, inner thighs, and the small of the back.

Stay in tune with what areas of your partner's body, and your own, are particularly or unusually sensitive, and make the most of them.

Take Some Initiative!

Often men feel that they do the bulk of the initiating, so they are beyond thrilled when their partners take on that role instead. If you make a point of taking the lead in your sex life with your partner, not only will he feel loved, wanted, and needed, but he will also be aroused by your take-charge attitude. As an added bonus, you will also find yourself aroused when you take on this role.

As most men will tell you, just the idea of a woman initiating sex is one of their absolute top turn-ons. So why not transform that sizzling hot fantasy into a reality for your lover? After all, when you initiate sex, you make him feel not just wanted, but downright irresistible! And who doesn't like to feel irresistible?

You will find it exciting and empowering to show him who is boss, even if you only do it once in a while. Remember, variety is the spice of life! So, considering how much fun it is for both of you, why not initiate sex more often?

Senses for Sex

You have five amazing senses with the capability of heightening your sexual desire to new levels, so use them! Make a point of being aware how things look, sound, smell, feel, and taste all the time. Human beings are sensory creatures by nature, and the way to turn us on, physically speaking, is to appeal to as many of our five senses as possible.

What You See Is What You Get

When it comes to physical turn-ons, as we have discussed, paying attention to your appearance still matters, regardless of how long the two of you have been together and how comfortable you are with each other.

The way you look in general, but especially when you are about to make love, can strongly stimulate your desire, and your partner's, too. Consider posing sexily or stripping for him, as both are wonderful ways to prolong your pleasurable pre-sex anticipation.

If it's a weeknight, and you don't have the time or energy to run through your whole beauty routine, do a couple of quick self-esteem boosters to help you feel attractive and appealing—brushing your hair and teeth, and putting on a touch of lip gloss are easy to do and rewarding. Investing a little time and energy in your appearance shows your partner that you still care about how you look, not just for him, but also for yourself.

Sounds Like Love

Playing sexy music can enhance your sexual desire. As Shakespeare wrote in the opening line of *Twelfth Night*, "If music be the food of love, play on."

Indeed, music has a powerful hold on many of us. We associate it with memories, both good and bad. To give you a sense of just how powerful music can be, think about how often you have been driving along in your car and when a certain song plays on the radio you find yourself transported back to a specific time of your life. This is how music and memory can work hand in hand to put you and your partner in a certain mood or state of mind.

Perhaps you and your partner have a special song, or even several songs that you consider "your songs." Maybe one of the songs is a slow, tender, romantic love one that was played at your wedding. And maybe another is a raucous rock tune you remember from the party where you first met. Or, you may always have a soft spot in your heart for a band that the two of you saw in your dating days. Replaying these songs at key moments can induce strong feelings of happiness, nostalgia and sexual excitement.

Knowing just how powerful (and how sexual) music can be, try to harness that power to enhance your sex life with your partner. Think about the music you both like, and think about the songs that make you feel sexy and in the mood for making love. When you are in the mood for love—or when you would like to get yourself in the mood—play the songs that make you feel your sexiest and most amorous. Then let the music work its magic.

In addition to music that turns you on, the sounds of pleasure that your partner makes during lovemaking can also be a powerful turn-on. When your partner moans, groans, and gasps, calls out your name, or says, "Yes, yes, yes," these are self-esteem boosters that are very arousing for both of you.

Love Booster

When you feel you are about to climax, you can help the process along by making arousing sounds. These actions will send your brain the signal that the time is right to climax, and soon you will have your orgasm!

As we discussed in "The Generous Gesture" section of Chapter 2, sometimes giving in the bedroom can be more exciting than taking, and the sounds that your partner makes when you are being sexually generous or just generally rocking his world can help maximize your own physical (and emotional) pleasure.

Scent of a Partner

The sense of smell, in a variety of ways, works invisible wonders as a sexual turn on. Like music, scents also can create and leave footprints on our sexual memory.

Taking a relaxing bath with your partner and breathing in fragrant bath oils can be deeply erotic and sensual, and when you take in this fragrance again you are reminded of a sensual experience you associate with that scent. Candles release a subtle, sexy fragrance into the air, and rubbing each other with scented massage oils are also ways to enhance sexual desire.

In addition, many people are turned on by their partner's perfumes, colognes, aftershaves, scented body lotions, or even just their natural scent. Men and women have been using fragrances to attract and keep mates since ancient times. Also, people can also be turned on by their *own* perfumes and scented lotions.

After all, much in the same way that wearing a sexy garment can make you feel attractive, wearing a special fragrance can boost your confidence, too. These two positive sensations—feeling sexy and confident—work in tandem to enhance your sexual desire.

Our discussion of scent and sexual desire wouldn't be complete without a brief look at the debate over human *pheromones*.

def•i•ni•tion

Pheromones are naturally produced chemicals that trigger specific behavioral responses in members of the same plant or animal species.

Thanks to an extensive amount of research, scientists are certain that pheromones exist in several plant and animal species. We know, for instance, that in certain animals, the females in the species emit sex pheromones to let the males know they are available for mating. What scientists are less certain of, however, is whether or not pheromones (and specifically sex pheromones) exist in human beings. More research needs to be conducted before they can know for sure either way.

Unfortunately, even though science has yet to establish whether or not human beings emit sex pheromones, over the past several decades, businesses with highly suspect motives have marketed products falsely advertised as "human sex pheromones" to take advantage of people's wishes to try almost anything to enhance their sexual desire or improve their sexual performance. Our advice on this is to wait for authentic scientific proof that human pheromones truly exist, and don't fall prey to false claims from scam artists—who are most likely clogging up your e-mail inbox with these fraudulent messages).

Touch Me, of Course!

Of course, one of the most effective tools couples have for enhancing sexual desire is their fingertips. Many people find that nothing drives them more wild and gets them more excited for sex than the intimate touch of their partner's hands.

Touching your partner's skin and hair during intimate moments and feeling her skin pressed against yours can recharge your sexual desire. Experiment with different kinds of touching, from soft, light, and tender to passionate and intense.

Run your fingers up and down the lengths of each other's bodies, and ask each other what feels particularly good. Revel in the profoundly sexy sense of togetherness that intimate touch always provides.

Rebecca Drury, an exotic dancer and the author of *The Little Bit Naughty Book of Lap Dancing for Your Lover*, teaches her readers teasing and titillating tricks to increase both sexual anticipation and passion. Sexy moves like the "grinding circle" and "the slap and tickle" are designed to drive you both crazy with desire. After all, a lap dance is the hands-on version of a striptease, and what could be better for building up your anticipation of what's to come?

> **Mood Killer**
>
> Closed off body language, downcast eyes or glum expressions can give your lover the sense you don't want to talk, kiss, touch, or make love, causing hurt and making him feel undesirable. Instead, be nurturing in your emotional and sexual intimacy giving lots of touch, eye contact, welcoming body language, and tender, loving facial expressions.

That Tastes Good

The taste of your partner's mouth and skin can be very exciting, which is one of the reasons that deep kissing is so effective for enhancing sexual desire. Of course, generally speaking, the tongue and the lips are both essential ingredients when it comes to making love with your partner because they are key erogenous zones (a topic we discussed earlier in this chapter).

But what about the more conventional meaning of "taste"? Yes, we mean in relation to food. And since all of us love food, it's wonderful to know that food can be an incredible source of sensuous pleasure.

Many people consider eating with their partners to be a part of their erotic repertoire. For instance, sharing a delicious dinner with your partner is a wonderful form of foreplay. Strawberries and champagne are widely considered a traditional part of any aphrodisiac feast. Other foods with a reputation for being potent aphrodisiacs or "foods of love" include oysters, figs, truffles, chocolate, and caviar. It is believed that these foods are capable of arousing not just your taste buds, but your bodies as well. So why not go out especially for oysters on the half-shell and a chocolaty dessert just for the sake of making love later.

Talk to Me, Baby

The private language that partners share can enhance their sex life in many ways. For starters, nearly all couples have special words that trigger erotic worlds just for them. For instance, maybe all you have to do is say "risky business" to invoke a whole slew of sexy (or poignant or funny) memories that the two of you share involving that particular movie.

Similarly, maybe you have always enjoyed talking your own private language of made-up words that have a special meaning for the two of you. These words or styles of speaking, such as baby talk, can form a significant part of your intimate bond.

Some couples like to talk dirty in the bedroom, peppering their sex talk with colorful, naughty, off-color words. Just keep in mind that this is one of the areas where both partners have to be on the same page. If talking dirty is not for you under any circumstances, it's important for your mate to know this, so that he does not risk offending you in any way.

For example, "Who is my naughty little sex kitten?" only works if you both dig that kind of talk. If only one of you enjoys it, naughty talk can end up being about as sexy as a lead balloon. This axiom applies equally to words that can be construed as misogynist or derogatory in most contexts.

On the other hand, if you and your partner both find it exciting to talk in an outlaw, boundary-pushing, taboo-shattering sort of way, then feel free to do so. Remember, sex-talk preferences are deeply personal. It's up to the two of you to decide what works and what doesn't.

Sexy, flirty conversation with your partner on a regular basis can not only enhance your sexual desire, but can also serve as a fun stand-in for sex. For instance, if the two of you are talking on the phone or having an e-mail exchange (on private e-mail accounts that no one else has access to, of course), you can always slip in a little naughty talk, just to give yourselves both a sexy energy boost during the day.

Remember, private language enables the two of you to recharge the undercurrent of sexual passion in your relationship. You're reminding each other that sex is always there, hovering between you as a wonderful possibility, just waiting for you to reach out and grab it.

As with everything else, the key is communication. Talk about these matters openly and honestly. When you both put all your cards on the table, sexually speaking, you will gain a deeper understanding of each other's sexual boundaries and turn-ons, which, of course, can only enhance your sexual desire and lovemaking.

An Occasional Change of Scenery

Making love in a different place, like a hotel, for instance, is a simple but effective way of shaking up your routine and adding some sizzle.

Alternatively, perhaps you and your partner like to make love in the great outdoors, under the stars or inside a cozy tent. What a wonderful way to commune with nature and with each other at the same time. And talk about a smorgasbord for the senses! There is something intensely romantic about listening to the night sounds, and smelling the crisp night air, while simultaneously tuning in to your mutual sexual needs and desires.

And let's not forget there are many rooms in the house worth exploring. The kitchen counter or table, the basement, the attic, or why not the back seat of the car in the garage!

There are many exciting places to have sex with your partner other than your bedroom. Don't be afraid to explore them.

Anytime Is a Good Time

If the two of you tend to have sex mostly in the evening, bear in mind that you can enjoy making love any time of the day or night. Think of the fun you can have stealing time for an afternoon quickie with your partner!

Love Booster

Having sex in the middle of the night can be raw, primal, and deliciously impulsive and unexpected, so why not give it a try?

The primary reason that variety of any kind (including a varied sex schedule) is stimulating is that it offers something new and fresh, a break from the usual routine. We like to be surprised—by good surprises, that is. And having sex at a different time of day that your usual time definitely falls into the category of a good surprise!

To put it another way, varying your sex schedule is fun and stimulating in precisely the same way that trying a new sexual position or technique is exciting. It's a change! And change can be a good thing, or in this case, a *very* good thing. And as we've been saying all along, anything at all that you and your partner do to keep things fresh, innovative and exciting in the bedroom is bound to enhance your sexual desire.

Tantric Sex

A few years ago, the English pop singer Sting was ribbed in the press for openly discussing his belief in the power of tantric sex. He and his wife of many years, actress and political activist Trudie Styler, had become devoted practitioners of it, which, he maintained, prolongs and improves lovemaking and orgasms. The fact is that many couples all over the world practice some personalized version of tantric sex. Many couples believe that it has elevated their sex lives (and their relationships in general) to whole new levels of emotional and physical intimacy.

If you and your partner are curious about Tantra and about the possibility of incorporating tantric lovemaking techniques into your love life, you may want to read *The Complete Idiot's Guide to Tantric Sex* for a helpful, informative introduction to the practice. Even if you don't become a tantric sex expert, you may find that some aspects of this ancient practice strongly appeal to you and your partner.

def•i•ni•tion

> **Tantric sex** originated in India and incorporates Yogic principles. Simply, it is about fusing sexuality with spirituality, with the ultimate goal of turning the physical act of sex into a sacrament of love.

> **❝❞ Notable Quotable** _____
>
> "Most of the techniques Marc and I use are tantric. In doing this
> work, it helps to have the vision of the Goddess and the Warrior.
> This approach helps the woman feel her femininity and the man his
> masculinity. It's really all about releasing one's power and letting go. This
> stuff can be very powerful and erotic."
>
> —Sally, 51

The Latest Scientific Research

Sex researchers are learning more and more about sexual desire and
the similarities and differences between men and women on what turns
them on sexually.

Arousing Findings

In the 1950s, renowned sex researchers William H. Masters, Virginia
E. Johnson and Helen Singer Kaplan proposed the following theory of
human sexuality: Most human beings experience a sexual thought (or
urge, craving or desire) which they then act upon with a partner, which
triggers the body to go into a state of sexual arousal, which leads to sexual activity, an increasing feeling of both pleasure and pressure, sexual
climax, and, finally, satisfaction.

But more recent studies, including those conducted by Ellen Laan,
Stephanie Both and Mark Spiering at the University of Amsterdam,
have illustrated conclusively that the body is actually not sexually
"wired" the way Masters, Johnson and Singer Kaplan once believed.

In a telephone interview conducted by _New York Times_ reporter Natalie
Angier for her comprehensive April 10, 2007, article on sexual desire,
"Birds Do It. Bees Do It. People Seek The Keys To It," Dr. Laan told
Ms. Angier, "We think that sexual desire emerges from sexual stimula-
tion, the activation of one's sexual system."

And as Angier points out, "The new findings also suggest that in some
cases, the best approach for treating those who suffer from low sex
drive may be to focus on enhancing arousability rather than desire—to

forget about sexy thoughts and emphasize sexy feelings, the physical queues or activities that arouse one's sexual circuitry. The rest will unwind from there, with the ease of a weighted shade."

In other words, the latest, up-to-the-minute sex research confirms that one of the best ways to enhance one's sexual desire is to engage in sexually arousing activities with one's partner, even if one is not feeling a great deal of sexual desire at the outset of the encounter. This approach is sometimes characterized by sex researchers and therapists as the "Just Do It" school of thought on enhancing sexual desire.

What Women Want

According to Angier's article, the latest research also indicates that throughout the world, "Men on average report having a higher sex drive than women, and women prove comparatively more variable in their sex drive." In other words, sexual desire in women tends to be a nuanced, complex, multi-layered, idiosyncratic and highly subjective phenomenon, and it will probably take scientists a very long time to fully understand it.

But toward the end of the same information-packed article, Barry McCarthy explains in his interview with Angier that researchers are finding that men's sexual desire is a complex, nuanced phenomenon as well. Specifically, he notes that, "As men and women age, they become much more alike in so many ways, including in their sexual desire." And he adds that as men grow older, they are relieved to no longer feel the same internal and/or external pressures to view themselves as what McCarthy terms, "the sexual master of the universe."

Regarding women's sexual desire in particular, Dr. Stephanie A. Sanders of the Kinsey Institute and Indiana University reported to Angier that she and her colleagues had recently assembled a series of women-only focus groups in which they asked the participants to describe in very precise language exactly what it feels like to be sexually turned on.

In Dr. Sanders' own words, many of the women "mentioned a heightened sense of awareness, genital tingling, butterflies in the stomach, increased heart rate and sensitivity, muscle tightness. Then we asked if they thought the female parallel to an erection is genital lubrication, and they said no, no, you can get wet when you're not aroused, it changes with the menstrual cycle, it's not a meaningful measure."

According to Dr. Sanders, 655 of the women who participated in these focus groups also completed a long sex survey for the Kinsey Institute. A fair number of their responses seemed to match up with some of the conventional wisdom about what turns women on sexually.

For instance, Sanders told Angier that "93 to 96 percent of the 655 respondents strongly endorsed statements that linked sexual arousal to 'feeling connected to' or 'loved by' a partner, and to the belief that the partner is 'really interested in me as a person'; they also concurred that they have trouble getting excited when they are 'feeling unattractive.'" Of course, these particular findings are in synch with what sex therapists and relationship experts have been saying for decades about how women experience sexual desire.

But when it comes to making finer distinctions regarding how women experience sexual desire, it turns out to be much harder to make sweeping, all-encompassing statements about what most women find sexually appealing.

As we discussed earlier in this chapter, our sense of smell can be an important part of getting physically turned on. But as it turns out, the scents that women enjoy and find sexually stimulating vary widely. Specifically, some women report that they feel turned on by a man who smells of body odor (i.e., perspiration), because they find the scent masculine and, therefore, sexually alluring. But other women who participated in the survey stated that they feel utterly repulsed when a male partner smells of body odor.

Also, conventional wisdom tells us that a woman's sex drive is nearly always severely dampened by stress or anger. But, at least according to the results of this recent Kinsey Institute survey described by Dr. Sanders, a solid quarter of the female respondents reported that they regularly use sex as a means of relieving stress, or sometimes even as a means of resolving a fight with their partner. (We were actually quite interested and heartened to learn of this particular statistic, because we agree that sex can function as a fantastic stress reliever and form of communication, not only for women, but for men as well.)

And finally, regarding the time of month when pre-menopausal women are the most likely to experience their highest levels of sexual desire, there is now a large body of research indicating that this peak moment occurs during or around ovulation. Most sex researchers maintain that it simply makes logical sense (both from an evolutionary and a reproductive standpoint) for women to feel a noticeable surge of sexual desire during the time of the month when they are most fertile.

The Least You Need to Know

- Sexual desire and arousal are all rooted in certain key physical activities, ranging from rubbing, kissing, touching, and massaging, all the way up to sexual intercourse.

- A strong physical sexual bond requires couples to commit to the exciting process of mutual discovery, and to talk openly and honestly about what they most enjoy in bed as well as what they might like to try in the future.

- Marital sex (or sex between partners who have been together for a long time) often gets a bad rap in the press and in pop culture. In reality, sex between two people who love each other very much and know each other very well can sometimes be the hottest, most rewarding kind of sex there is.

- Tuning in to all five of your senses before and during your lovemaking can significantly enhance your sexual desire and pleasure.

- Talking dirty, having sex at different times of day and in new locations, and initiating sex more often can all be physical turn-ons.

- Research indicates a correlation between a woman's sexual arousal and their feelings of love from and connection to their partner.

Chapter 5

Emotional Turn-Ons

In This Chapter

- ◆ Trust and safety are the building blocks of true emotional intimacy
- ◆ Emotional intimacy and sexual intimacy are like opposite sides of the same coin
- ◆ Some emotional turn-ons, like warmth, confidence, and emotional stability, are true for everyone
- ◆ When it comes to making love, the journey is as exciting as the destination
- ◆ Love gestures like writing love notes are preliminaries to enhancing sexual desire

A happy, satisfying marriage or long-term relationship ideally consists of equal parts sexual intimacy and emotional intimacy. Both may ebb and flow over time, but neither can vanish completely if the relationship is to thrive.

Think of emotional turn-ons as your partner's particular personality traits and actions that rub you the right way on an emotional level. On the other hand, think of physical turn-ons, generally speaking, as everything we covered in Chapter 4, especially your partner's physical characteristics and seductive behaviors that automatically trigger your feelings of sexual desire.

In this chapter, we will focus on emotional turn-ons, paying specific attention to what they are (including universal emotional turn-ons), and how they can foster both emotional and sexual intimacy. We'll also look at the touching literary portrait of emotional intimacy of Calvin and Alice Trillin. And we'll explore how expressing your appreciation for your partner, both with your words and your deeds, can strongly enhance not only your feelings of emotional intimacy, but also your sexual desire.

The Building Blocks of Love

The key to enhancing your sexual desire is figuring out how to feel more connected to—or more emotionally intimate with—your partner. Bearing this in mind, be aware that there are certain important prerequisites or building blocks that must be in place for emotional intimacy to grow and flourish.

For starters, both partners need to trust each other completely. In fact, without trust, there can never be authentic emotional intimacy. There has to be healthy, nonjudgmental, mutually accepting communication between partners. In addition, both partners have to feel safe, both emotionally and physically, in each other's presence.

Once two partners have established these key prerequisites, mutual self-disclosure can take place. Think of this as the verb form of emotional intimacy, or emotional intimacy in action. Mutual self-disclosure involves sharing whatever is in your hearts, as well as feeling totally relaxed and accepted after the sharing takes place.

Emotional intimacy is sometimes difficult to establish and maintain because it often involves revealing our deepest personal secrets. Any time we disclose our innermost thoughts and feelings, or stories about our more troubling past experiences, we feel vulnerable.

And for some people, feeling vulnerable (even with someone they love and trust) can be overwhelming and upsetting, because they may equate feeling vulnerable with being weak or cowardly. Men are particularly susceptible to this feeling, but women can sometimes feel it, too.

If you struggle with the idea of revealing your softer, more vulnerable side in the presence of your loving partner for fear of judgment of weakness, take confidence in knowing that doing this is actually the very opposite. It shows tremendous emotional strength and courage.

We all need to be able to feel emotionally intimate (i.e., emotionally naked and vulnerable) around our partners. Why else would we be with them? In fact, this is such a profound human need in love relationships that when it is lacking, it can signal the beginning of the end of the relationship. When emotional intimacy is missing, one or both partners may end up seeking it in the arms of another lover.

Most of us are not born with an innate understanding of how to be emotionally intimate. In addition to the building blocks of trust, communication, and safety, emotional intimacy requires practice. You may think that confiding openly and honestly in your partner ought to come naturally. And perhaps it does for those who have always been surrounded by loving, supportive, positive, nurturing relationships.

But for others, particularly those who have grown up in dysfunctional families or who have been in emotionally abusive love relationships, feeling safe and the abilities to trust and communicate in a positive way may not come so easily or naturally.

For such individuals, being in a loving, supportive relationship, perhaps for the first time in their lives, will take getting used to. It can also take a fair bit of time and practice. Fortunately, once you get the hang of communicating with your mate openly and honestly, chances are you will start to cherish your new intimacy. When that happens, being direct and above-board with your partner will begin to feel perfectly natural, almost as if you've been in the habit of practicing emotional intimacy your whole life.

If this is your first nurturing love relationship, you should be proud of yourself. A life-affirming part of your core being has steered you in the right direction. This inner drive, along with your ability to overcome obstacles from your past, says a lot about you, not just in terms of your resiliency and emotional survival skills, but also in terms of your belief in yourself and the healing power of authentic love.

Building up and continually practicing your emotional intimacy skills with your partner will deepen your self-awareness, your self-knowledge. After all, sometimes we don't fully grasp our own innermost thoughts and feelings until we write them down in a journal, or say them out loud to someone we trust. So think of your emotional intimacy with your partner not only as a means of feeling close and enhancing sexual desire, but also as a significant part of your journey to a fuller understanding of yourself.

Remember, it can be challenging to allow yourself to experience your full range of feelings—especially painful emotions such as anger, fear, sadness, frustration, heartache, or grief—and even more challenging to express these feelings constructively and sensitively to your partner. But true emotional intimacy is the miracle that enables you to face all of your feelings head-on, and in so doing, be fully accepted. This is the connection we are all seeking. Indeed, when you make the decision to know your partner and to be known by your partner, you will find that the two of you occupy common ground. You will also find yourself gaining fascinating insights into *all* of your relationships, not just your relationship with your mate, but also with friends and family members.

The Ultimate Emotional Turn-On

Feeling safe, supported, and fully loved and known by your partner is perhaps the ultimate emotional turn-on. To feel known—*really* known, inside and out—is to feel deeply loved and accepted, and these feelings of *emotional intimacy* can enhance your feelings of sexual desire for your partner.

def•i•ni•tion

> **Emotional intimacy** means that you and your partner are willing to reveal your innermost turn-ons, sexual and emotional desires, dreams, hopes and fears to each other. This can be a challenging proposition, even in the most loving and trusting of relationships. We all long to feel totally safe, accepted and not judged by our partners, especially after we have actively engaged in emotional intimacy by exposing some aspect of our innermost selves.

However, the relationship between emotional intimacy and sexual intimacy is complicated. It requires the two of you to strike a delicate balance between these two equally important forms of intimacy. All couples must find their own unique way of striking this balance.

Two helpful ways to understand the complex interaction between emotional intimacy and sexual intimacy are to view it either as two sides of the same coin or as Yin and Yang.

The concept of Yin and Yang, which is rooted in ancient Chinese philosophy, holds that two complementary yet opposing primal forces are found in nearly all noteworthy ideas or phenomena throughout the known world. (Yin traditionally represents the feminine, receptive force, while Yang typically stands for the masculine, active force.)

Notable Quotable

"At its core, marriage is a respectful, trusting friendship that requires emotional and sexual intimacy to thrive. A marriage ... cannot survive without touching and emotional connection."
—Barry and Emily McCarthy, *Rekindling Desire: A Step-by-Step Program to Help Low-Sex and No-Sex Marriages*

Your Personal Intimacy Style

In the previous chapter about physical turn-ons, we discussed the sorbet rule as one way of thinking about how to mix, or, as the case may be, how not to mix, sexual intimacy with emotional intimacy. Of course, this rule is not hard and fast: the sharing of sexual fantasies can lead directly to making love, or it may not. Nor is it the only variable to consider when deciding how to blend (or how not to blend) these two equally important sides of the intimacy coin.

Indeed, there are at least two additional factors to consider when it comes to the question of whether or not to directly mix emotional intimacy with sexual intimacy: (1) the larger context in which a particular private moment between you is taking place, and (2) your personal intimacy style as a couple.

For instance, let's say that your husband's work friend has just been in a relatively serious car accident. The friend is going to be fine, but your husband has just come home from visiting him in the hospital, and the visit has visibly shaken him. Right now the two of you are alone in your bedroom and the kids are asleep, so you have total privacy. But what you choose to do with your alone time says a lot about your personal intimacy style as a couple.

On the one hand, your husband may just want to cuddle and talk about how visiting his friend in the hospital made him feel. And he may not be at all interested in mixing this intimate conversation and cuddling time with sex. On the other hand (remember Chapter 3 and the various roles sex can play in relationships), he may view sex—particularly the slow, tender kind of lovemaking—as a source of solace when he is upset, and affirmation and even thanksgiving for his life. If this is the case, he may want to combine emotional intimacy with sexual intimacy in a more direct way, using your time together first to share his feelings about the hospital visit and later to make soft, gentle love.

> **Love Booster** _____
>
> An emotionally intimate relationship enables you to intuit each other's emotional needs and desires, read each other's body language, and develop a sixth sense for knowing when the time is right for talking, or for quiet, communal togetherness or for making love.

Universal Emotional Turn-Ons

An attractive face and a fit body are considered universal physical turn-ons by just about everyone. But emotional turn-ons are important, too, because so many people look for these qualities when choosing their mates. Here is a list of personality traits typically considered universal emotional turn-ons:

- Commitment/stick-to-it-ive-ness/persistence
- Fidelity/sexual faithfulness/trustworthiness
- Intelligence/intellectual curiosity
- Willingness to praise/reticence to judge or criticize
- Emotional stability/internal fortitude
- Willingness to compromise and seek common ground
- Confidence/strong self-esteem
- Warmth/generosity of spirit
- A good sense of humor
- Kindness/tenderness

> **Mood Killer**
>
> People who are cold, distant, closed off and unwilling to engage in genuine emotional intimacy do not make good partners, and they are not likely to change. Seek out a potential mate who is warm, open-hearted and emotionally giving right from the beginning.

Calvin and Alice

An inspiring account of what profound emotional intimacy between authentic soulmates can look and feel like, read *About Alice*, by Calvin Trillin, an affectionate, exquisitely written remembrance of his late wife and muse, Alice Stewart Trillin, who died in 2001. The eternal love Trillin felt (and clearly continues to feel) for his beloved Alice beautifully illuminates every word of his spare but elegant prose.

It's not so much a portrait of private grief over the loss of a beloved spouse, in the way that Joan Didion's memoir of losing her husband John Gregory Dunne, *The Year of Magical Thinking*, is. Although Trillin's grief is a significant part of the book's poignancy, it's more the celebratory story of what Trillin himself calls "the transformative power of pure, undiluted love." For instance, in recalling the many pieces he wrote for *The New Yorker* that included tender, funny stories about Alice, Trillin writes, "… I got a lot of letters like the one from a young woman in New York who wrote that she sometimes looked at her boyfriend and thought, 'But will he love me like Calvin loves Alice?'"

A reviewer for *Newsday* suggests that the book is such a moving, powerful testament to the undeniable power of love that people ought to give it to their newlywed friends as a wedding gift, with an accompanying note that says, "'This is how it's done.'"

Still, many reviewers and readers of the book have characterized the Trillins' marriage as the kind of love (and intimacy) that is achievable only by a select few, not by most of us.

Well, we beg to differ.

We believe that the emotional intimacy the Trillins shared in their long, happy marriage is glorious and worth celebrating. But we also believe that everyone can strive for an equally deep connection with his or her partner. After all, being the kind of partner you want to be boils down to making a conscious and consistent effort to not just put your best foot forward, but also put your best *self* forward, and expecting your partner to do the same.

Making Babies

While the procreative role of sex is not the main focus of this book, we would be remiss if we did not mention it at all, because some couples never feel closer (emotionally or sexually) than they do when they are actively working on conceiving a child. In other words, when making love not just for mutual physical and emotional pleasure, but also with the intention of creating a brand new life together, some couples feel happier, more emotionally fulfilled, and more powerfully bonded to each other than ever.

The baby-making period of your relationship can also be a very liberating and, therefore, sexually exciting time for you and your partner. After all, you don't have to worry about birth control, perhaps for the first time in your lives! You can have sex any time, anywhere, on the spur of the moment, with absolutely zero anxiety about getting pregnant, because getting pregnant is now your shared goal. And you know what we always say about anxiety and lovemaking—the less of it you have, the hotter the sex!

It's the Journey, Not the Destination

Many people make love with one goal in mind: reaching orgasm. And of course, it's undeniably great to experience physical satisfaction during sex with your partner. But orgasm need not be the only goal, or even the most important goal of your lovemaking. Remember, intimacy is also about feeling close to each other, emotionally as well as sexually.

There's no doubt about it, orgasms are great! They relieve stress and leave you feeling deeply relaxed. But focusing on the journey of lovemaking rather than on the destination of orgasm can bring the two of you closer (emotionally and sexually) than anything else you do as a couple. Going on this love journey together, as an intimate, loving team, is more important, and perhaps more rewarding, than one or both of you achieving orgasm every single time you make love.

It's particularly important to remember that while some people have orgasms every single time they have sex, others (particularly women) do not. So when you both make the conscious choice to focus less on having orgasms and more on the lovemaking journey, you are taking a lot of pressure off both of you and enjoy it more.

Think about it. Asking yourself, "Will I or won't I have an orgasm this time?" can really drive you crazy and suck a lot of the joy and spontaneity right out of the moment. So instead, why not tell yourself: "I can't wait to feel our bodies pressed together. We always feel so close and connected when we make love."

Actions Speak Louder Than Words

Words are great, especially words like "I love you" and "You mean the world to me" and "You look so hot and sexy." But when you and your partner show each other how much you mean to each other, this can pay off for both of you in countless ways. Emotional turn-ons in the form of love habits or rituals can foster your emotional intimacy and keep things cooking in the bedroom!

Some couples make a tradition of reciting their wedding vows to each other, perhaps once a week or once every other week. This is a particularly touching way to let each other know how much you still care. It can also serve as a powerful means of reinforcing your feelings of emotional intimacy.

Leaving love notes for each other all over the house is another popular way to stay close. You can tape notes anywhere: on your home computer, your bathroom mirror, or inside a briefcase or purse.

The notes can be as innocent or as frisky as you like, from the simple "You mean the world to me" to "You totally turned me on last night!" Also, you can establish a special place that is sacred to the two of you, somewhere that is your sanctuary of happy memories. Maybe the two of you have a special greasy-spoon diner that holds particularly sentimental value for you both, or a park bench where you first kissed. Or the place where the two of you had your first date, or where you decided it was time to start a family. No matter what, it ought to be a place that both of you hold dear. Whatever the reason, keep going there as one of your ongoing rituals.

Many couples love to cook together, perhaps not every night—most people don't have that kind of time—but as often as their schedules will allow. Remember those foods of love, those yummy aphrodisiac edibles we mentioned in the previous chapter? Perhaps the two of you can find some clever, exciting ways to incorporate some of these sexy ingredients into the love recipes you whip up together as a dynamic duo.

Also, many people who love to cook say that it relaxes them and sends them to a happy place, emotionally speaking. You know what we like to say about sex and relaxation: The more relaxed you are, the better the sex, and the better the sex, the more relaxed you are!

Expressing Appreciation

Everyone needs to feel appreciated by their partners on an ongoing basis in order to feel sexual desire, arousal, and satisfaction. Conversely, those who feel underappreciated, taken for granted, or completely unappreciated by their partners are not likely to have much interest in having sex with them.

Often it's the simplest gestures of appreciation that mean the most. The random, totally unexpected offer to pick up the kids from school, cook dinner, or give a massage or foot rub add up to so very much over the course of time.

Many relationship experts and marriage counselors espouse the "relationship bank account" metaphor as a helpful way to think about your love partnership. It's a reference to the supply of positive relationship energy the two of you have "banked" in your relationship.

Every time the two of you put your personalized love habits into practice, or say or do something nice and selfless for each other, think of it as putting a fresh deposit of good energy and goodwill into your relationship's emotional bank account. Any time you check in with each other by phone during the day, smile at each other, wish each other well, or give each other kisses, back rubs, or pats on the bottom, you are expressing your appreciation for your partner and your relationship, and are building strength in your emotional bond.

The Domino Effect

Remembering "the Generous Gesture" we discussed in Chapter 2, this story illustrates the domino effect of big-hearted and selfless gestures. Recall from that story that Marian decided to put her never-ending chores aside one night and, instead, seduce her husband Jim.

Well, this one change of plan on Marian's part ended up setting off an extraordinarily positive chain-reaction that neither she nor Jim could ever have expected in their wildest dreams! Not only did Marian's unexpected act of seduction make Jim happy, but it inspired him to want to pitch in more around the house, which, in turn, made Marian happy.

But Marian wasn't only grateful for Jim's renewed interest in helping out around the house. She, also, and this is a biggie—surprised herself by finding out how much she had enjoyed seducing him, and by how much she loved the sex!

Simply put, Marian's seduction of Jim, while it was giving him something he really wanted, actually did more to reawaken her sexual desire—which had been lying dormant for quite some time—than anything else she had tried in the past. Before that fateful night, she hadn't realized how much she had lost touch with her own sensual nature. By giving to Jim, she actually gave to herself, tenfold! Clearly, this one simple act of seduction and lovemaking revitalized Jim and Marian's relationship in different, equally important ways.

Past Sexual Experiences

A big part of emotional intimacy involves the ability to talk about tough subjects, including past sexual experiences. Communicating about sexual issues or concerns can be particularly challenging. It can feel strained and awkward, even for couples who have been together for a while, and who are generally open and honest about everything else in their lives. Sometimes, however, talking about potentially touchy sexual subjects is necessary for the health and growth of your sexual and emotional relationship as a couple.

Concerning the past, many notable sex experts, including sex therapist and author Barry McCarthy and his wife and co-author Emily McCarthy, have noted that a majority of men and women have had at least one negative sexual experience in their past. This experience has caused them to feel ashamed, humiliated, or, in some cases, perhaps even violated. It bears mentioning, however, because although everybody's past experiences color their present ones in many ways, two loving, compassionate partners can work on healing and recovering from this particular pain together.

There are two ways to begin the healing process: showing and telling. By showing, we mean you ought to give your loving partner the chance to show you (as often as possible) just how pleasurable sex can be with someone who is caring and nurturing. And by telling, we mean that there may be times when you will want or need to talk to your partner about what happened to you in the past.

Talking with your adoring mate about any negative past sexual experiences you may have had can help you in a variety of ways. For starters, it can give you the chance to vent your anger and pain to a safe person in a safe setting. Second, it gives your partner the chance to listen to you, validate your anger, and let you know you are perfectly justified in feeling the way you do. And finally, it gives you both the opportunity to let each other how know how safe, loved, nurtured, and protected you both feel now.

Of course, if there is anything deeply traumatizing from your sexual past that is still causing you significant emotional pain and suffering to this day, we strongly recommend professional counseling. A therapist who specializes in trauma can help you work through your pain and move past it. Therapy can also help you to feel safe, whole, and happy again. You will be able to fully enjoy all aspects of your current relationship, including your sex life. (We will address this important subject of sexual trauma and how to seek treatment for it, again in Appendix B.)

Trouble in Paradise

Even when things are going well overall with you and your partner, and you're connecting, talking, sharing, and having fun, sometimes things still just might not totally click sexually. If this happens sometimes, or even more than sometimes, there is no need to panic or get too stressed out. Instead, remember that when the two of you work together as a loving team, you share the power to make changes for the better. So, if there are certain changes you'd like to suggest, take a deep breath and consider using some of the specific communication strategies we describe below.

As we have discussed, sex is one of the key ways that you communicate as a couple. If something is not working in your sex life, you need to let your partner know about it. For example, if what used to stimulate you no longer does, talk about it. Or, in fact, if something she's always done has never aroused you, let her know about it. Also, let her know when something she is doing feels good, and the things she does that always make you feel good.

This communication needs to be made in the least-hurtful, most-constructive way, paying close attention to how you word your feelings. For instance, instead of saying something potentially hurtful or con-frontational like: "You're doing that all wrong," instead, say in a loving way: "Honey, I love that you're trying something new, but it's a little uncomfortable for me. How about if we tried this instead."

You can always redirect her from a sexual activity you aren't particu-larly enjoying by saying something like, "You know what I really love is when you ...." Fill in the blank with one of your reliably favorite sexual activities.

Many people prefer not to talk about what's not working in the bed-room when they're in the middle of making love. That's okay, too. They may instead want to discuss the situation outside of the bedroom, albeit in another private setting. Perhaps when the two of you are alone in the car together or taking a walk will work better for you.

The location of the conversation is less important than having the con-versation. When you do address the problem, be sure to use the kind-est, most encouraging words you can think of. You want to resolve the issue quickly and amicably, so that you can both resume fully enjoying your lovemaking as soon as possible. Also, please don't keep your secret sexual desires a secret. Take a risk. Share your sexual secrets with the one you love, and show excitement when he tells you his.

Mood Killer

Being sad, sick and/or physically or emotionally exhausted can take the desire out of sex; and while these feelings are normal and you can't help them sometimes, don't let these feelings or circumstances disconnect you from your partner. And on your "off" days, never forget the power of cuddling!

Taking "the Long View"

Emotional turn-ons evolve differently than physical turn-ons in several important ways. For instance, your physical turn-ons are deeply personal. You may feel powerfully aroused when your partner strokes your thigh, as it may be one of your hot spots or erogenous zones. But you may feel only tender affection (rather than sexual arousal) when your mate whispers sweet nothings in your ear. Or you may have the exact opposite reaction.

In addition, your physical appearance gradually changes over time, and so does your mate's. Part of maintaining or enhancing your sexual desire as the years go by is learning how to adjust to and accept these changes.

So keep in mind, something that physically turned you on at age 20 may not have the same arousing effect on you at age 30, or it may return when you're 40! It's important to pay attention to the evolving nature of your sexuality as you mature in age.

In contrast, emotional turn-ons can be less subject to change. Chances are if you felt emotionally turned on in your 20s by a guy who is kind, generous, hard-working, verbally expressive, and willing to commit, you will still feel that way in your 30s, 40s, 50s, 60s, 70s, and beyond.

When it comes to both physical and emotional turn-ons, it's helpful to "take the long view." What does that involve exactly? Well, as an example, let's consider a fictional couple named Amy and Joe. When they first got together, Amy was physically turned on by Joe's muscular, athletic physique. Twenty years have now passed. Joe's physique is still attractive to Amy, but admittedly he is no longer quite as buff as he was when they first met.

Now, if Joe's fit physique was the only thing that Amy loved about him, this could potentially be a problem. But most people who stay together for 20 years share an attraction that is not only physical, but is also emotional. In other words, they share an attraction that is built to last, and is not likely to be torpedoed by one or both partners putting on a few extra pounds around the middle.

Also, many other things have been going on during their 20 years together. For instance, maybe Joe has seen Amy through a long, drawn-out grieving process following the early, unexpected deaths of both of her parents. And maybe Amy has helped Joe muster up the courage he needed to make a major midlife career change, a change that has brought him great professional and personal satisfaction. And maybe they have shared the experience of having a child together who has made their lives feel complete.

When you consider the larger context of this relationship, you can see why Joe's having gained a few extra pounds over the years would make absolutely zero difference in the love that he and Amy share. If anything, their love—including their sexual attraction—has grown and deepened over time.

If the present-day Amy were to meet the younger, buffer version of Joe, the Joe she initially fell in love with, she would probably still find him as handsome and charming as ever. But she would probably also see him as naïve, unschooled in the realities of life, and not nearly as attractive to her—physically or emotionally—as the more mature, seasoned, and worldly man she shares her life with today.

Paying attention to the ever-evolving nature of your love relationship, both physically and emotionally, remembering the strong emotional ties and turn-ons that keep you together contributes to the long-term view and health of your sexual desire.

The Least You Need to Know

◆ Emotional intimacy and sexual intimacy can be seen as two sides of the same coin, or as Yin and Yang, two opposing yet complementary forces, both of which are necessary for a healthy love relationship to thrive.

◆ The main building blocks of true emotional intimacy are safety, trust, and strong communication. This combination leads to emotional intimacy in action, or the mutual sharing of your authentic selves.

◆ Some people struggle with the idea of emotional intimacy, and fear that exposing their true feelings will be construed as a sign of weakness. In reality, a willingness to be emotionally intimate and vulnerable with your partner is a sign of courage and inner strength.

◆ When it comes to emotional turn-ons, remember that actions speak louder than words. It's important to express your appreciation for your partner in a variety of ways, both big and small.

◆ When you take the long view, you realize that your emotional connection with your partner will help carry the two of you through all of life's joys and challenges.

Chapter 6

Feeling Sexy

In This Chapter

- ◆ Feeling sexy, vibrant, and in touch with your sensuous side enhances desire and passion
- ◆ Positive self-talk enables you to love yourself inside and out
- ◆ The unattainable images glorified by the media
- ◆ Mirror meditation helps you get as comfortable as possible in your own skin
- ◆ Sexy eating and living habits lay the foundation for more frequent and more satisfying lovemaking

Liking yourself and feeling good about your body are potent aphrodisiacs. A big part of enhancing your sexual desire has to do with feeling good and taking pleasure in how you look and feel. When you feel attractive, your energy level, self-esteem, and body image improve dramatically, as does your sexual desire. On the other hand, when you are feeling down on yourself for any reason, it can be a challenge to feel sexy and to experience sexual desire. Feeling sexy begins with sensual living.

Fortunately, if you are struggling with issues that make you feel down, such as low self-esteem, poor body image, or low energy, there are a variety of practical, easy-to-implement steps you can follow, some physical and some emotional, to feel sexier, happier, and better about yourself that will also enhance your overall level of sexual desire.

Get Comfortable with Yourself

There are many different ways to boost your confidence and get comfortable with yourself. In this section, we'll discuss caring for your skin as a great way to feel sexy and enhance sexual desire and confidence. We'll also explore how you can learn how to love your body and feel sexy, strong and self-assured at any age.

Skin Is In

Skin is an erogenous zone, one of the many parts of your body that when touched and caressed elicits sexual arousal. From your skin and hair, to your neck and ears, to your fingers, the small of your back, the backs of your knees, right down to your toes, all your tiny body parts, all those exciting little erogenous zones make you feel alive. To be alive and enjoying yourself is the essence of desire.

Sensual living is erotic, and a big component of your eroticism is your skin. Taking care of your skin can mean using lotions and creams that make you feel hot, sexy, and full of sexual desire, through their aroma, how they make your skin feel, and even the act of applying them on your body. It feels sexy and healthy to have soft, smooth skin all over. Getting a facial, pedicure, or a massage whenever the mood strikes you can also make you feel good about yourself. You are not being selfish by practicing healthy body care. On the contrary, you are making the choice to live a sensual, erotically charged life.

Sexy at Any Age

Aging well is sexy and appealing. If you practice sensual living and self care, you will improve with age! Think about all the ways women get better with age—they get wiser and focus more on how they feel inside, rather than on what's sagging. If you continually pay attention to your authentic sensual nature and your feelings of sexual desire and sexual pleasure throughout your years, you will age gracefully, joyfully, and very sexily.

Best of all, with age comes not only wisdom, but also a lifetime's worth of priceless experiences that are uniquely your own. So, if you keep your focus on taking care of and being good to yourself—mind, body, and soul—you'll be comfortable with yourself and your body no matter what your age.

A big part of feeling sexy at any age is rooted in your sense of sexual self-confidence, and this comes from within. It's absolutely fantastic when you have a partner who makes you feel good about yourself by encouraging you, paying attention to you, complimenting you, kissing you, caressing you, etc. But ultimately, *you* are responsible for empowering yourself and for building and maintaining your own positive self-image, no matter what your partner is or isn't doing or saying to you.

Some people mistakenly equate confidence with arrogance, or they think low self-esteem is the same thing as humility, but these comparisons are inaccurate. When a person is humble or modest it doesn't necessarily mean they suffer from low self-esteem. Rather, they don't feel the need to brag about their accomplishments. And when someone is conceited or arrogant, they have an excessive amount of confidence—as opposed to a healthy amount—and an over-inflated sense of their own importance and worth.

Having a healthy, well-balanced sense of self-confidence means that while you don't think you're infallible or perfect, you do have a generally positive view of yourself. That is, your self-image is essentially good, but it's also grounded in reality, so that it's neither not too high nor too low. For instance, when people say, "So-and-So just has that special spark, that inner glow that makes her radiantly beautiful both inside and out," they are talking about someone who believes in herself and has a strong, solid core of healthy self-confidence.

If you sometimes (or even constantly) struggle with low self-esteem (particularly in the sexual arena), as many people do, the good news is there are several practical steps you can take to boost your sexual self-confidence. When you feel confident, you also tend to feel sexy and alluring. And as the very latest sex research indicates (remember from the end of Chapter 4), when you feel sexy, you tend to have a greater desire for sex.

Without further ado, here are sexy confidence-building tips to help you increase both your self-esteem and your sexual desire:

◆ Think about all the sexual goals—both big and small—you have set for yourself *and* accomplished. For instance, if you don't usually initiate sex in your relationship, or are shy about wearing sexy lingerie, but you did recently a time or two, add these to your mental list of accomplishments, and feel good about them. Contemplate all the positive feelings you experience when you achieve these sexual goals. Maybe initiating sex made you feel proud of yourself, strong, in charge, sexually assertive hot and powerful. Allow these self-empowering words to sink deeply into your consciousness so they can become a permanent part of how you feel about yourself.

◆ Set additional sexual goals. To continue with the previous example, maybe now that you've initiated sex and worn sexy negligee, next time you have sex with your partner, try sharing a favorite fantasy, or suggest having sex in a different room or at a different time of day. Over the course of time, these accomplishments start to add up and you will feel like a brand new, infinitely more sexually confident person.

◆ Keep your goals reasonable and achievable. For instance, perhaps even during the honeymoon stage of your relationship, you were not someone who wanted to have sex every single day. Therefore, it wouldn't make sense to set daily sex as one of your sexual confidence-boosting goals. In fact, we don't advise setting any of your sexual confidence-building goals around sexual frequency. When it comes to enhancing your sexual confidence and desire, your enjoyment of your sexual relationship with your partner is far more important than the actual number of times the two of you have sex.

◆ Reward yourself—ideally with a sensual, body-celebrating prize— such as getting a manicure-pedicure or massage. As we have said, when you feel sexy all over it kicks off a sort of sexy feedback loop. By this we mean when you build up your sexual confidence by achieving one or more of your sexual goals, and you then reward yourself with a fun, sensual prize that makes you feel even sexier, you will likely feel all the more eager to accomplish yet another of your sexual goals. One sexy step feeds into the next, which feeds into the next, until a fantastic little desire-enhancing circle or loop is formed.

♦ Take your cues from confident people in your life or in the public eye. If you know people who appear to have just the right level of self-confidence, observe them in action and take mental notes on what they say, how they behave, and how they present themselves to the world. Or, take notes on how well-known people who exude a quiet but genuine sense of self-confidence carry themselves. It can be helpful to observe celebrities who have been in the public eye for decades, who are still considered as sexy as they were at the beginning of their careers (if not even more so), and who keep finding interesting projects to work on (despite the very real age bias that exists in Hollywood). Some sexy, vibrant women who spring to mind—all of whom are over forty-five, and, in some cases, over sixty—include Helen Mirren, Diana Ross, Meryl Streep, Angela Bassett, Christie Brinkley, Susan Sarandon, Lauren Hutton, Connie Chung, Charo, Goldie Hawn, Blythe Danner, Cher, Diane Keaton, Michele Pfeiffer, Gladys Knight, Sally Field, Sharon Stone and Catherine Deneuve.

♦ Reciting daily affirmations or mantras can be a helpful tool for boosting self-confidence and enhancing sexual desire. The trick lies in coming up with one that works effectively for *you*. For instance, your daily mantra could be something as simple and straightforward as repeating the words, "I feel strong, sexy and confident today," five or ten times in a row each morning after you have brushed your teeth.

♦ Act confident even when you don't feel particularly confident. This is not about being fake, it's about overcoming negative feelings of self-consciousness in order to put your best foot forward. Surely those sexy female celebrities we listed above have days when they don't feel so great about the way they look. And yet, because they make their living in the entertainment industry, they need to conduct their public lives according to the showbiz adage, "The show must go on." that could drag them down.

Turning Lemons Into Lemonade

When your level of sexual desire is not as high as you would like, it can be easy to get discouraged. When faced with a personal challenge, such as low sexual desire, some people able to soldier on until they find a solution, whereas others seem more inclined to feel defeated and give up.

Salvatore R. Maddi, a psychologist and researcher, set out to find the answer to this and related questions, including: "Why are some people so good at turning lemons (i.e., negative situations) into lemonade (i.e. positive outcomes)?" Or, to put it another way, "Why do some people seem to be so good at bouncing back or rallying during and after a challenging experience?" And finally, "Even if this ability to bounce back is an innate personality trait in only some of us, is it also a skill that can be learned by anybody, given the proper training?"

Dr. Maddi conducted a 12-year longitudinal research study of a group of people who were coping with a massive, extremely difficult change in their workplace.

His findings, published in the scientific journal *Consulting Psychology Journal* in 2002, indicated two-thirds of the people he studied did not cope well with the challenging situation, developing a variety of physical and mental health problems, as well as performing poorly at their jobs. But notably, one-third of the group actually seemed to excel during this extremely trying time in their work lives.

When Dr. Maddi interviewed the people who were performing with the proverbial grace under pressure, he found they seemed to share three important beliefs about life. These beliefs consistently enabled them to turn lemons into lemonade, regardless of the nature of the problem they were facing. In the mental health field, individuals who display this innate character trait are considered emotionally resilient or emotionally hardy.

In his own words, Dr. Maddi describes the problem-solving approach of the emotionally hardy individuals in his study as follows: "**Commitment**, **Control** and **Challenge** attitudes. The **Commitment** attitude led them to strive to be involved in ongoing events, rather than feeling isolated. The **Control** attitude led them to struggle to try to influence outcomes, rather than lapse into passivity and powerlessness.

The **Challenge** attitude led them to view stressful changes, whether positive or negative, as opportunities for new learning."

Here are Dr. Maddi's three main findings further defined:

1. Hardy people, or people who manage to thrive during and after difficult times possess what Dr. Maddi calls a "Commitment Attitude." As soon as they are faced with a challenge, they throw themselves into making things better right away, and they stay committed to making things better until they accomplish this goal.

2. In addition, rather than throwing up their hands in despair and declaring they have no control over the difficult situation, they assume a "Control Attitude." They refuse to be passive and let the problem take over their lives. Instead, they make up their minds they can have at least some control and influence over the tough situation, and they have the ability to change it for the better.

3. Finally, these hardy folks also manage to maintain a "Challenge Attitude" during rough patches. They tend to view the difficult experience as a challenging learning opportunity, rather than as something that is ultimately going to defeat or overwhelm them.

Dr. Maddi found that most emotionally resilient people seem to share a positive, can-do attitude that enables them to keep difficult periods in their lives in perspective. They appear to have a profound, gut-level understanding of the old saying, "This, too, shall pass." They also have managed to develop a useful repertoire of effective coping skills that help them keep their cool both during and after periods of moderate to severe adversity.

Simply put, they *believe* with all their hearts they can and will feel better one day, in spite of the negative experiences they are currently going through. This belief gives them the hope and emotional nourishment they require to actually *make* their lives better.

Once his research confirmed that some people are indeed innately emotionally hardier than others, Dr. Maddi posed the following questions: "Can less hardy people become hardier and more emotionally resilient than they are now?" In other words: "Can more emotionally vulnerable people train themselves to develop thicker skins so they can become more skilled at enduring—and then moving beyond—life's hardships and challenges?" And finally, he wanted to know: "Can emotionally vulnerable people actually learn how to *thrive* in the face of adversity?"

We are pleased to report that Dr. Maddi's research answers each of these questions with a resounding "Yes!"

In fact, after gathering all of his data (which included interviewing all of the study participants at length), Dr. Maddi ultimately used his findings to design a course for people who would like to become hardier. If you are interested in learning more, visit www.hardinessinstitute.com.

So how can these learning points help you deal with the problem of diminished sexual desire? Perhaps you feel you are in a tough spot right now with respect to your current level of sexual desire. And perhaps you believe your diminished desire is having a negative impact on your relationship with your partner.

If so, you will find it beneficial to embrace the Commitment-Control-Challenge attitude of Dr. Maddi's emotionally hardy group.

For a more specific example, let's say that you and your partner are struggling with a sexual desire gap. You generally desire less sex, whereas he generally desires more sex. How exactly might you apply Dr. Maddi's Commitment-Control-Challenge attitude to your gap in sexual desire?

Start by making a commitment to boost your sexual desire. Remember, emotionally resilient people are profoundly committed to resolving their problems. They throw themselves into finding solutions, and keep trying until they find the particular solution that works for them. They may struggle and get frustrated at different points along the way. But what makes them emotionally resilient and generally successful in achieving their goals is they keep trying, making adjustments as necessary, until they achieve success.

Next, take control of the situation. Throughout this book, we talk about everyone's need to take charge of increasing their own sexual desire, not only for the sake of their intimate relationship with their partners, but also for the sake of their personal well-being. Sex is not everything in a love relationship, but it is important. When sex disappears (or almost disappears) from a couple's relationship, it generally does not bode well for their future together. Sex is an indicator of the overall health and intimacy level of the relationship. So "seize the day" by taking control of enhancing your sexual desire, rather than allowing it to slip away.

And finally, along with *committing* yourself to finding a solution and seizing *control* of the situation, consider viewing your quest to enhance your sexual desire not as an insurmountable hardship, but rather as a *challenging* learning opportunity for personal growth and development. Be patient, gentle and encouraging with yourself. And to avoid feeling overwhelmed—or feeling like giving up if you experience setbacks along the way—remember that making genuine, lasting, worthwhile change in any aspect of your life takes good will, time, patience, commitment, hard work and—perhaps most important of all—a generous helping of humor.

Self-Acceptance

Some things about our bodies we simply can't change, nor should we try! Instead, accepting your unique curves, characteristics, and shape of your body enables you to feel sexy in your own skin and love your body.

Let's look at an example of a 25-year old woman named Maggie who has only recently started to appreciate her body. It has been a long, hard journey. When she was 7 years old, a boy in the playground called her chunky, and ever since then, she has felt self-conscious about her looks in general, her weight in particular. While she never succumbed to full-blown eating disorders during her teen years, she did go through brief periods when she dieted, lost some weight, but then gained it back.

According to the scale, her weight during adolescence was always in the normal range for her height. Still, she had many days when she looked in the mirror and longed to have a body type closer to that of her best friend Joanna. Joanna studied ballet and had always been told by dance teachers and coaches that she had "the perfect body for ballet," meaning, of course, that from early childhood on, she had always been slender and petite.

These days, Maggie is in a happy, monogamous relationship with a young man named Luke. They recently became engaged, and she is looking forward to planning their wedding. One of Luke's most endearing qualities, at least in Maggie's eyes, is his unabashed love of her voluptuous figure. He adores her full breasts and hips, and constantly tells her, and shows her with displays of private and public affection, exactly how much he enjoys her curvaceous shape.

Happily, Luke's ultra-positive opinion of Maggie's body has rubbed off a bit on her. Indeed, he has helped her to view her figure in a brand new, more positive light. In all honesty, she still has moments here and there when she flashes back to high school, and briefly experiences that old longing to be a size 2.

But nowadays, she mostly likes the person she sees in the mirror. Her new appreciation of her figure has made her both desire (and enjoy!) sex more than she has at any other time in her life. Of course, meeting and forging a relationship with the right partner helped renew her sense of sexual pleasure as well. But Maggie is convinced that her recent boost in self-esteem has been an equally important factor in enhancing her feelings of sexual desire.

Last, but certainly not least, while it's fun and exciting to feel that lovely surge of confidence when your partner (or anyone else) pays you a compliment, it's also important to remember that genuine, lasting self-confidence and self-acceptance come from within. In other words, it's fine to enjoy the praise of your partner and others, but it's not emotionally healthy to expect or rely on external praise as your sole or most meaningful way of boosting your morale and self-confidence. When people become emotionally autonomous by believing in themselves and taking charge of boosting their own confidence—rather than relying on others to do it for them—that's when they evolve as human beings.

> **Notable Quotable**
>
> "Confidence is the sexiest thing a woman can have. It's much sexier than any body part."—Aimee Mullins, gold medalist Paralympic athlete, actress, model, bilateral amputee.

Those Voices in Your Head

Virtually all of us engage in an ongoing internal monologue throughout our lives, and it plays a big part in shaping who we are and how we feel about ourselves. Therefore, it makes sense to give these monologues as upbeat a spin as possible, to learn how to develop skills in "positive self-talk."

Maggie can help us understand this concept. Here's the old Maggie engaged in negative self-talk: "I'm so mad at myself. Why did I have that second bowl of ice cream? I'll never fit back into that pretty dress Luke likes me in so much. How does he put up with me? Why can't I look like those women on T.V., the ones with the perfect bodies and faces? He claims I'm still as sexy to him as ever, but how can that be? I feel like I've let myself go these past few years. If I keep eating at this pace, Luke will feel totally repulsed by me in no time flat."

The new Maggie looks at the same situation with a very different viewpoint: "It probably wasn't a great idea to eat two bowls of ice cream. I'm smarter than that, and I'm definitely capable of making much healthier choices. So from now on, that's exactly what I'm going to do—make healthier eating choices.

"Luke is such a wonderful husband. He loves me and desires me sexually whether I gain a few pounds or lose a few pounds. In his eyes, I'm perfect and desirable just the way I am. So I'm going to take this cue from him and go a little easier on myself. I made a mistake. I wouldn't be human if I didn't. Next time I will listen to my body, and when my body tells me I'm content, I will pay attention. After all, my sweet tooth was more than satisfied after I ate that first bowl of ice cream, so there was no need to eat the second one. Live and learn."

When Maggie talks to herself in this positive manner following her minor lapse in judgment, she is accomplishing several things. First, she is reminding herself that she is married to a great husband who loves and desires her unconditionally, who always finds her hot and sexy, no matter what the scale may say on any given day.

Second, she is treating herself with gentle compassion and forgiveness. While it's great to set high (albeit reasonable and achievable) expectations for yourself, it's never a good idea to demand perfection. After all, no one is perfect, so why set yourself up for failure?

Third, Maggie is letting herself know that just because she made this mistake, there is no need for her to make the same mistake again in the future. She recognizes that mistakes are valuable—they are teachers.

Fourth, she is telling herself that she is smart and perfectly capable of making better eating choices going forward.

It's helpful to remind yourself that (1) life is full of choices, and (2) more often than not, you will make the right choice.

> ### Notable Quotable
>
> "Remember, it's easy to default to a negative self-opinion. We all do it some of the time. Today is the day to begin actively being positive. The more you practice, the simpler it will become and the more natural it will feel."
>
> — Eve Salinger, author of *The Complete Idiot's Guide To Pleasing Your Man*

Your Voice of Sexual Desire

Your ongoing personal monologue is even more important when it comes to your sex life. People who are gentle, encouraging, complimentary, and compassionate with themselves are likely to derive the most pleasure from their sex lives. On the other hand, people who tend to be harsh and overly critical of themselves are less likely to desire or enjoy sex.

As Maggie has shown us, you have an enormous amount of power over your own moods and feelings. Depending on what you say to yourself from minute to minute, you can make yourself happy or sad, stressed or relaxed, angry or forgiving. Remember, you are your own greatest and most valuable life coach. Be as positive, constructive, and motivating as possible when it comes to your internal monologue, your body, and your sexuality.

Of course, it's not always as easy as it sounds to be positive. If you are concerned that your ongoing personal monologue is too negative too much of the time, here are concrete tips and strategies to help you make your internal monologue more positive, both in content and tone.

> ### Mood Killer
>
> A big part of being a good lover and good friend to your mate comes down to loving the person you are, loving the skin you are in, and loving yourself. Accepting yourself enables you to be kind, loving and nonjudgmental with other people, including your partner.

Open-Minded And Open-Hearted

Keep an open mind. What if your partner suggests a new idea, perhaps an erotic scenario he would like to try in bed? For instance, maybe he would like to role play a delivery man and you the frisky housewife, or he'd like to make love in an unusual place or new way.

As long as it is within reason to you, rather than trying to talk him out of it, try using positive self-talk to talk yourself into it. You may surprise yourself and discover you really enjoy it. Remember, nothing ventured, nothing gained!

Blame Is Lame

If something doesn't go according to plan in the bedroom, it can be tempting to blame one's partner for what went awry.

Don't play the blame game with your partner (or anyone else for that matter). People sometimes use blame as an easy way out of an uncomfortable situation.

For example, if one partner suggests trying a new sexual technique, but the experience doesn't go smoothly, there's no need for either partner to blame the other for the less-than-perfect lovemaking session, especially considering that not every sexual experience can be stellar. Blaming one's partner is really an avoidance of assuming any personal responsibility in the situation, and it's hurtful and deconstructive. After all, in the above scenario, one partner was open enough to suggest something new, and, therefore, should not be blamed or criticized if it doesn't turn out as planned.

Instead, when you encounter trying circumstances, use strategic and logical self-talk to figure out what *you* might have done differently to help achieve a more positive outcome.

Mood Killer

Blaming each other when problems arise in your relationship is not helpful. By assuming personal responsibility, rather than assigning blame, you will find satisfying solutions to problems *together*.

The blame game gets you nowhere and can be debilitating to your sex life. Actively taking responsibility for your part and working toward a solution is the way to go.

Avoid Negative Terminology

During your waking hours, your internal monologue never takes a vacation, not even when you are in bed with your partner. So, when the two of you are thinking about having sex or are engaging in sexual activity of any kind, keep your self-talk as uplifting as possible.

Stay away from negative thoughts like, "I look so fat in this negligee" Or "I'm getting older and I don't look the same as I used to. Why does he still want me?" Instead, say things to yourself like, "I feel curvy and womanly in this negligee. I love the sexy way it clings to my skin. And from the way he's acting, I can tell he loves it, too!" Or "Wow. Our relationship has really stood the test of time. We've been making love for so many years now, and he still wants me. Every time we make love it feels fresh and new."

"Absolutely," Not!

Steer clear of what mental-health experts call "thinking in absolutes," a cognitive style that is marked by frequent use of phrases such as "always" and "never." This un-nuanced kind of thinking fails to take into account the countless shades of gray that exist between "always" and "never." In the example of your partner wanting to try out a new erotic scenario in bed, rather than telling him, "I would never agree to acting out that kind of sexual scene," consider rephrasing it like "That sounds intriguing. Just let me think about it first." This second response is much gentler, much more positive, and considerably more encouraging. It shows your mind is open, you don't want to shoot down his idea or hurt his feelings, and you will, at the very least, consider his suggestion. When you open your heart and mind to new sexual possibilities, it can boost your interest in sex.

Don't "Should" All Over Yourself

Many of us are in the habit of telling ourselves we "should" do this or that, and this can be a very unforgiving way to live. To avoid the harsh, dictatorial notion of "should," simply replace it with "could."

For example, when you tell yourself "I could initiate sex more often," rather than "I should initiate sex more often," it sounds much gentler and less judgmental.

The Sky Is Not Falling

When people find themselves in a particularly negative frame of mind, often as a result of engaging in too much negative self-talk, they can find ways to do what mental-health professionals refer to as "catastrophizing."

They take a situation that is relatively minor—you want to make love, your partner doesn't—and turn it into something monumentally horrific. This kind of thinking that blows things way out of proportion is neither rational nor fruitful, and typically does not have a positive outcome. Try to hang onto your sense of humor, as well as your sense of perspective. And don't make a big deal out of small, temporary, resolvable issues.

Low Expectations

Some people believe that it's a good idea to keep their expectations low and assume the worst is waiting for them around the corner. In this way, they will be pleasantly surprised if the worst does not come to pass. The problem with this approach is that they're always thinking in negative rather than positive terms.

More than anything else, thinking in a negative manner leads to pointless stress and anxiety. So instead of saying to yourself, "No matter what I try, I won't be able to increase my sexual desire," try saying, "There are so many different ways to enhance my sexual desire that I just know one or more of them is going to work great for me."

Quit Complaining!

Some people whine and complain constantly, often out of habit. They complain to their partners, friends, family members, and colleagues, and they even complain to themselves! For some people, complaining has become an integral part of their ongoing internal monologue.

Unfortunately, complaining all the time keeps the focus on our problems, rather than on exploring ways to *solve* our problems. We have to figure out ways to be solution-oriented rather than problem-oriented in our thinking style.

For instance, it's easy (but not constructive) to tell yourself "My level of sexual desire has been declining steadily over the years. That's just the way it is, and there's nothing I can do about it."

But it's so much more motivating to tell yourself "At the moment, my sexual desire may not be quite what it was when I was 20, but I know there are many ways to foster my feelings of emotional intimacy with my partner, and explore with him the wonderful world of physical and emotional turn-ons."

Mirror Meditation

Appreciating your beauty, accepting yourself, and knowing that you are attractive are the gateways to a vibrant life. Here is a simple meditation that will get you pulsating with self-acceptance. Practice it daily, and in a month you may find that you are less self–conscious about your face and other body parts. You might even notice a fresh glow and sparkle in your eye, because when you gently look at yourself without judgmental comparisons, you uncover the secret about how lovely and vital you really are.

Schedule five to ten minutes of uninterrupted time for this meditation. Try to do it at the same time each day so that it becomes part of your beauty routine. Consider fitting the meditation in before or after a shower.

Dim the lights, light a few candles, and play soft, relaxing instrumental music—whatever works to set the tone for you to focus on you. Sit in front of a full-length mirror. Begin the meditation draped in a soft blanket, a towel, or robe. Gaze into your eyes and notice their shape and color. Some people say that the eyes are the window of the soul, so take as much time as you like and look deeply. Relax your shoulders and allow tensions to melt away. Relax your mouth.

Notice your facial features, your hair, the shape of your nose, your lips, and ears. Soften your eyes and smile kindly at the image in the mirror. When you are ready, drop your robe and look with ease at your entire body. Slowly gaze at all your body parts from your neck to your breasts, to your waist and abdomen, to your pelvis, hips and thighs, to your knees, ankles, and feet. When you have looked at every little part, bring your gaze back to your eyes. Smile at the image in the mirror and give her two thumbs up, or make up your own signal of love and acceptance of what you see.

Many women report that when they look at themselves tenderly they discover a full range of characteristics that they hadn't acknowledged before. Oh sure, you may see blemishes here and there, but those blemishes fade in the background when you become familiar with how lovely a womanly body can be. Some women report that after a week of practicing this mediation they just naturally shed a few tears over the cruel things they have thought about their lovely bodies. Others report that sweet laughter bubbles up from their bellies as they experience the joy of self-acceptance for perhaps the first time. These are positive voices of your sexual desire.

Remember, smiling at yourself is the joyous expression of being alive. We suggest that every time you pass a mirror or see your reflection in a window that you give yourself a knowing glance and smile.

By the way, when you have mastered this meditation, you might consider introducing it to your partner. However, in place of the mirror, the two of you will gaze at each other. You might be pleasantly surprised at how much delight and happiness spring forth when you take a moment to look directly into the eyes of your lover.

Media Mistruths

The media is rife with images of unattainable perfection, images that seem deliberately designed to make people feel bad about themselves. Even sexual activity is generally depicted in a wildly unrealistic fashion onscreen. It's important to examine how media images can damage people's self-esteem and address what people can do to fight these negative influences, while simultaneously safeguarding their own precious emotional health and well-being.

Perfect Body Image

Many women—and men, too—struggle with body-image issues. Women can think they are too curvy, too fat, too skinny, too flat-chested, or that they have too much cellulite. In fact, so many women aspire to look like the supermodels who grace the cover of *Sports Illustrated* that plastic surgery procedures (such as breast augmentation and liposuction) have sky-rocketed in recent years. According to the Plastic Surgery Research Information Center, between 1997 and 2005, there was a 444% increase in the number of cosmetic procedures. That's a lot of nipping, tucking and augmenting!

Speaking of *Sports Illustrated* cover models, television talk-show host and supermodel Tyra Banks, who, in 1997, was the first African-American model to grace the magazine's cover, decided in early 2007 to do a photo shoot wearing the exact same bikini she wore for that original cover. She's as gorgeous as ever, but in the 10 years that have passed since the original cover photo, she put on roughly 30 pounds.

As she told a reporter who interviewed her for the February 18–25, 2007, issue of *TV Guide*, "I want to empower women to not stress about what they see on the scale. I am 161 pounds. I say it loud and proud. My breasts are fuller, my thighs are fuller, my waist is fuller, but to me it still represents beauty."

They're Not So Perfect After All

Many people, mostly women, also fret about the appearance of their face. They might say to themselves, "Why doesn't my skin glow like So-and-so's on the cover of Cosmopolitan?

First and foremost, the media is saturated with lies, optical illusions, *"Photoshopping"* and airbrushing, especially when it comes to depictions of female beauty. Indeed, as part of her admirable mission to help women feel better about themselves, Tyra Banks would probably be the first person to tell you that no one, not even actual movie stars and fashion models, look in real life the way they do on magazine covers or on screen.

def•i•ni•tion

Photoshopping refers to digitally manipulating and editing photographic images. The term originated from the name of the graphics software program used to do this, "Adobe Photoshop." Using this software, a graphic designer can take an original photographic image of a model and manipulate it to make someone appear considerably thinner than he or she actually is and his or her skin look inhumanly flawless. Altered versions of photos are what we see in most magazines and advertisements.

Movie stars and models get blemishes and crow's feet and dark circles under their eyes, just like everyone else. It just so happens that when they go to photo shoots and movie sets, ultra-flattering lighting and teams of stylists, make-up artists, and photographers work tirelessly to make them look flawless.

For example, in the television ad for Dove's "Campaign for Real Beauty," a lovely but down-to-earth and real-looking woman is transformed, bit by bit, via make-up and extensive Photoshopping into a perfect sex goddess, whose final flawless image is then plastered on a billboard. The problem is, in the end, that image wasn't really her; it was not real.

In light of all this damning evidence, if you ever feel the slightest temptation to compare yourself in any way to these phony images of beauty in the media, please remind yourself that it's all totally fake, a big con job, every last bit of it.

Reality Is Not the Movies

We all are constantly being bombarded with media images and ideas pertaining to sex, and female sexuality in particular. But these images have little to do with real life. On television, in movies, and in romance novels, sex is nearly always depicted as some wild, violently passionate, rip-each-other's-clothes-off scenario. In real life, while sex can certainly be exciting and passionate, it rarely resembles these cinematic acrobatics or literary scenarios. So it's important not to let these images shape the way we think about making love, our sexual desire, or what it means to feel and be sexually desirable.

There's actually a plus side to the discrepancy between media depictions of sex and real-life sex—it would be difficult and unproductive, not to mention exhausting, to live 24/7 at that torrid level. It would be expensive, too. Just think of all the clothes you'd constantly be buying to replace the garments you and your partner would be tearing to shreds during your love bouts!

Try not to waste too much of your precious time comparing your sex life to the kind of sex you see depicted on screen. If you get a new idea for something to try, great! But not even the actors and actresses playing the sexy parts are buying what they're selling.

Sexy, Sensual, and Healthy Living Habits

Feeling sexy and living that essence in your day-to-day life takes attention to habits that invoke your sensual nature. French Women Don't Get Fat, by Mireille Guiliano, is a book with many interesting morsels about how healthy eating is actually part of a larger plan to live a more sensual, pleasurable life.

For instance, she is a big fan of drinking lots of water. What exactly is so sexy about drinking water you ask? Well, for starters, when you keep your body properly hydrated by drinking eight to ten glasses of water each day, you are not just quenching your thirst, you are also moisturizing, cleansing and softening your skin from within, as well as improving your muscle tone. Water detoxifies your body by removing waste. In fact, when you drink enough water, you flush out toxins that might otherwise escape through the skin, causing breakouts and/or other skin problems. As we discussed at the beginning of this chapter, when your skin looks clear, and feels soft and supple, you feel sexy and attractive. And of course, feeling sexy and attractive is one of the most effective ways to boost sexual desire.

Guiliano also promotes eating organically grown fresh fruits and vegetables (such as strawberries and tomatoes), though only in season, when they are their tastiest. Indeed, eating fresh, seasonal fruits and vegetables can be a truly sensual experience. For instance, when you sink your teeth into a perfectly ripe tomato at the height of its season, you can awaken all five of your senses. The color, the taste and the aroma are out of this world. And the sound of your teeth ripping through the delicate skin, along with the feel of those delectable juices dripping down your chin, are nothing short of naughty.

For the record, *French Women Don't Get Fat* is not on every reader's list of favorite books. Some critics and readers have described it as "pretentious" and even somewhat "condescending" toward its intended audience. Nonetheless, we still think it contains an interesting, deeply sensual perspective on eating and life in general, and is worth a read to see for yourself.

Guiliano contends that French women don't believe in deprivation. If you crave a piece of chocolate or a glass of wine, have it. Just don't go overboard. In other words, she subscribes to the age-old philosophy of moderation in all things. Eating in moderation enables you to satisfy your craving for something sweet or salty without hating yourself for it afterward.

She readily concedes that the French famously enjoy their cheeses, breads, rich sauces, and any number of other tasty treats. But she also points out that they have a healthy sense of portion control. Also, the French (generally speaking) walk and bike just as a natural part of the course of their lives.

In her book, she includes weight-managing tricks and tips that French mothers have passed down to their daughters for generations. For instance, she espouses a detoxifying program that is comprised mainly of leek soup, which is to be consumed over the course of a weekend. And she is a proponent of eating food slowly, so as to savor every bite. For example, it's best not to scarf down a banana in 10 seconds flat. She advises cutting it into little slices, and chewing each one slowly and mindfully, in order to best enjoy the flavor of the fruit.

She is concerned that, too often, non-French women get caught up in faddish diets that can cause them to gain weight rather than lose it. She maintains that if American women could learn to view eating as one aspect of a lifestyle that is devoted to celebrating the senses, they could make some great strides toward conquering their weight issues, both real and imagined.

You could argue that her tips, as handy as they may be, are simply common sense wrapped up in lovely Parisian packaging. After all, she is a slim, attractive French woman, with an almost palpable joie de vivre and jet-setting lifestyle, who also just happens to be the CEO of her own champagne company. It doesn't get much more glamorous than that, does it? So maybe when glamorous Ms. Guiliano delivers these essentially common sense messages, more people are inclined to listen. At least this would appear to be the case, since this book, published in 2004, was a bestseller.

The Sensualist's Approach to Living

Mireille Guiliano is probably most accurately described as a "sensualist," or an expert in mindful, sensual living (she makes no claims to be a trained nutritionist.) Guiliano and sensualists like her teach us that we need to feed all of our senses, not just our sense of taste, equally well in order to feel truly satisfied.

For instance, she urges readers to keep vases filled with fresh cut flowers in various rooms throughout their homes. As a feast for both our eyes and our noses, flowers feed our senses and spirits.

Further evidence of her love of sensual, mindful living, Guiliano talks about different ways to wear a scarf. Now, in the greater scheme of things, is knowing a dozen different ways to wear a fashionable scarf a vital life skill? Is it going to help our collective quest for world peace? Well, not exactly. But, to a sensualist like Guiliano, it's these little touches and flourishes that add vividness, color, and panache to our sometimes-mundane, sometimes-challenging lives.

So why not at least consider heeding the advice of the sensualists, and give yourself little daily gifts of color and joy? After all, it is when we are paying full attention to the small but sensual details in our lives that we are living in the most mindful way. And it is when we are living mindfully that we feel the most attuned to our feelings, including our feelings of sexual desire. Not only that, but mindful living is what enables us to live in the moment, to be emotionally present, both to our partners and to ourselves.

Sexual Desire and Comfort Food

There is a powerful link between food and sex. Both arouse our senses, pique our appetites, give us pleasure, and ultimately make us feel satisfied. But sometimes, it's possible to confuse a desire for sex and emotional intimacy with your partner with a desire for food. So, if you want sexual passion with your partner instead inches on your waistline, pay close attention to what your body is truly craving.

You've heard the expression "comfort food" to describe foods that are filling, satisfying, tasty, and, more often than not, fattening. We sometimes seek these types of food for emotional comfort rather than the need for physiological nourishment. Eating more mindfully involves asking yourself: "Is what I'm feeling right now genuine physical hunger, or is it really sadness, thirst, fatigue, or a just a need for some fresh air and a little break? Or am I feeling a desire for more sex and intimacy with my partner?"

Evelyn Tribole, MS, RD, and Elyse Resch, MS, RD, FADA, are chief proponents of the "intuitive eating" movement (www.intuitiveeating. com) that advocates a similar position. Their book, *Intuitive Eating* talks about how so many people (particularly women) have been on so many different restrictive diets throughout their lives—diets that restrict carbohydrate, protein, or caloric intake—that they actually lose track of how to read their own body's need and cues about whether they are truly hungry, pleasantly full, or too full. This particular approach is interesting because it offers people a wide variety of tips for how to stop dieting and resume eating in a healthier, more self-aware manner.

For example, on their website and in their book, Tribole and Resch suggest "making peace with food." They maintain that people who diet for long periods of time often become overly punitive with themselves for eating certain foods. They further contend if people completely forbid themselves from having a particular food, they will only start to crave that food more intensely, a craving that can ultimately lead to binge-eating.

They also tell their "Intuitive Eating" clients to "respect their fullness." This involves really tuning into (and heeding) what their own bodies are telling them about their level of fullness. When they feel comfortably full (rather than *too* full), this is a good time to stop eating.

Another tip from Tribole and Resch involves teaching people how to comfort or reward themselves in ways that don't involve eating. In other words, sometimes people eat in response to feeling anxious or lonely, when more effective ways to combat these upsetting feelings might be to exercise, or call a friend, or (in keeping with the theme of this book), reach out to their partner to make love.

As Tribole and Resch suggest, asking yourself a question like, "Am I genuinely hungry or not?" can be a useful exercise and self-educational tool. Sorting through your emotions and tuning in to what you are *truly* feeling can lead you to a revelatory epiphany—maybe you don't really want that piece of cake sitting on the counter.

When you tune in to your true emotions using your inner monologue, you'll discover that what you actually want is not cake at all, but some cuddling—or perhaps even more than cuddling—with your loving partner.

Sexy Food Habits

Remember, food and sex are two of life's most potent sensual pleasures! Food is such a central and public part of our lives, it deserves attention to understand how even in the most routine areas of your life you can make choices that feel good and actually fuel your sexual desire.

Meal Time

First, eat slowly to achieve a few key healthy and sexy goals. Taking your time with your food fills you up with less and will help you avoid that uncomfortable and guilty feeling of being overly full. Plus, eating slowly is an incredibly sensuous act. This is one example where some movies get it exactly right! (Think $9\frac{1}{2}$ Weeks.)

Eat breakfast each day. A healthy, filling breakfast that is high in fiber can help you manage your weight and give you the energy burst you need to start your day on the right foot.

On days when you and your partner's schedules permit, consider feeding each other a healthy, sexy breakfast in bed! Afterward, you may want to linger there for a while to make love.

Next, make lunch your biggest meal of the day. You can control your weight more effectively, feel sexier, and enhance your sexual desire best by consuming the bulk of your calories during the day (when you need them most!), rather than in the evening.

If you and your partner enjoy making love in the evening (as many people do), eating a lighter supper will make you feel lighter and more comfortable when it's time for sex! Also, some people give themselves an eating cut-off time each day of two to three hours before going to bed. For example, Oprah says her cut-off time is 7:30 P.M., because she likes to go to bed at 10:00 P.M.

Remember, if your belly is too full from a filling dinner, you may not feel as much sexual desire. So giving yourself a cut-off time can give you a feeling of lightness and sexiness that will fill you with desire for making love with your partner.

Love Bites

Sexy foods like fruits and veggies are great for your skin, your waist-line, and your sex drive. Low in calories as well, fruits like strawberries, grapes, and melons make a sexy, juicy treat for two. Not only that, but they are also full of nutrients, so you can feed them to each other and feel great about eating them!

Speaking of fruits, didn't Eve seduce Adam with an apple? Apples, ahhh, the fruit of temptation! Feed your partner and yourself an apple a day and see where it takes you. Eat an apple as a light, sexy evening snack. Remember, every time you and your partner make healthy eating choices, like feeding each other apple slices in bed, you are not only making choices that are good for your health, but you are also making choices that are wonderful for enhancing your sexual desire and your sexual enjoyment.

As we alluded to earlier, eating fresh fruit happens to be a particularly sensual dining experience. For example, think about how it feels to bite into a fresh peach, the sensation of your teeth cutting through the soft, fuzzy outer skin and into the sweet, juicy, pulpy flesh that lies within. Remember how that delicious, tangy fragrance hits you like a wave, and how wonderful the peach's tart yet sweet juices taste and feel on your lips and tongue. Talk about seeing (and smelling and feeling and tasting) your food in a brand new, much sexier light!

Some say that the way to a man's heart is through his stomach. Well, we have been assured by hundreds of women that the quickest way to get romance started is with a good piece of dark chocolate! A piece of dark chocolate will satisfy your sugar craving and get the endorphins working so that you don't feel the desire to binge later on high-calorie sweets. Paying attention to the details of good nutrition, the smell, taste, look, and feel of your foods is sensuous, erotic, and pleasurable. Think of sexy eating as a form of foreplay!

Oysters, a shrimp cocktail, artichokes, avocados, almonds, asparagus spears, a platter of fruit, figs, and dark chocolate all have strong reputations as "sexy foods." Also, the taste and smell of almonds are known to ignite a woman's sexual desire and passion. And throughout the ages, honey, nuts, cinnamon, and other spices have all been considered powerful aphrodisiacs.

Mindful Beverage Consumption

Overindulgence in food or drink can dampen sexual desire and performance. People are sometimes unaware of how many calories they are consuming each day in liquid form. If you are currently a big soda drinker, think about replacing sodas and other sugary drinks with plain water, carbonated water, skim milk, or other low-calorie beverages. Please note that many fruit juices contain a surprising amount of calories. There's no need to be punitive with yourself or to totally eliminate fruit juice from your diet, only to limit your daily fruit-juice consumption to keep feeling sexy and full of desire.

One great trick is to begin each meal with a low-fat or no-fat appetizer such as a glass of water, a cup of soup or broth, or a salad. Remember, feeling light on your feet, sexy, and spry is great for enhancing your sexual desire and pleasure!

Preparing Sexy Meals Together

Remember that cooking together is romantic and sexually exciting. Just think of all the sensual chopping, dicing, stir-frying, sautéing, and tasting you can do together! Some couples love to cook a sexy meal together on their date nights. In fact, many couples find that their love life takes a turn for the better when they make their evening meals together.

Grocery shopping together for a meal you and your partner will prepare together is another sexy aspect of food and eating. Fill your shopping cart with ingredients that will make your sex life lively and fun. Spoiling each other by cooking and eating sexy foods together is not only an invitation to making love, but it's also easy on the waistline, and it will leave you both feeling satisfied and in the mood for having a sexy adventure together.

As you can see, when you spice up your life together in the kitchen, you may end up spicing up your sex life as well. So make your food preparation sexy and fun and all about intimacy and connecting. Turn off the television and turn on some sexy music. Set the table with candles, or have a picnic in front of the fire.

Almighty Exercise

Exercise is another way to feel healthy, sexy, and in touch with your body. And the wonderful thing is, sex, along with everything else that it is, is also exercise … great exercise. But exercise in other forms is also important for feeling sexy and to the sexual stamina you have in the bedroom. Let's discuss how they all fit together to enhance sexual desire.

Get Your Heart Pumping

As we discussed earlier, sex and other cardiovascular or aerobic exercises elevate your energy level and your endorphins (your sexy, feel-good hormones).

Love Booster _____

If sex and exercise are two things you and your partner could both use more of, why not combine the two? Start the evening by taking a romantic, moonlit walk together, and cap off the night by taking each other to bed.

When you exercise and are active, your body will be in better shape and you will feel more attractive, which can only boost your self-esteem and increase your sexual desire and drive. What could be better!

So consider running, biking, hiking and/or swimming, because all of these are fantastic forms of cardiovascular exercise that will both relax you and increase your energy level. And as we have been discussing throughout the book, the more relaxed and energized you feel, the more you will desire sex!

Two particularly informative exercise websites worth visiting are www. acefitness.org, the official website of the American Council on Exercise, and www.thebestlife.com, the official website of respected fitness expert Bob Greene, who is probably best known for being Oprah's personal fitness advisor.

Flex Your Muscles

Strength training involves performing a series of repeated movements (more commonly known as "reps") and the use of free weights, elastic bands, or weight machines. This type of exercise enables you to isolate and strengthen one specific muscle group at a time.

Strength training can boost your metabolism and build up your muscle mass while at the same time reducing your body fat, increasing your muscle strength and endurance, and improving your sense of balance and coordination. Like cardiovascular exercise, it will make you feel better about yourself and give your sex drive a potent boost.

What's important to remember about strength training is that it's best to start slow. Wait 24-48 hours between strength-training workouts, and don't exceed three strength-training sessions per week.

From a desire-enhancing perspective, strength training makes you feel muscular, sexy and more confident. In fact, it actually alters the shape of your body, causing your muscles to look more sculpted, toned and defined. And as we discussed earlier in this chapter, anything you can do to boost your confidence, improve your body image, and feel sexier and more attractive can work wonders for increasing your sexual desire.

Stretch for Sex

Stretching exercises, such as yoga, Pilates, and tai chi can help you avoid self-injury by elongating muscles, improving flexibility, and reducing stress. It's a good idea to stretch before and after cardio exercise or strength training.

Stretching is a particularly sensuous form of exercise because it is slow and relaxed, and it puts you in touch with your whole body. And when you elongate your muscles through stretching, you surely will feel leaner, more limber and sexier … and definitely more interested in making love with your partner! Also, the more flexible, graceful and in touch with your body you feel, the more inclined you might be to try out different sexual positions and/or techniques with your partner.

All sorts of stretching is good for your body, but certain stretching exercises can be particularly effective for increasing your flexibility and boosting your sex drive. Here is one sexy example to try for your inner thighs: sit on the floor with the bottoms of your feet pressed together and your knees dropped toward the floor. Slowly bring your torso forward until you feel a gentle tension in your inner thighs. Hold the position for a count of five and then release.

Good Slumber Makes for Great Sex

Sleep deprivation and chronic fatigue are arch enemies of sexual desire. If you want to enhance your sexual desire and increase your sexual pleasure, take heed of your need for healthy, uninterrupted sleep each night, typically $7^1/_2$ to $8^1/_2$ hours for most people. This need is as real and powerful as your need for food, water, clothing, and shelter.

Not only can chronic fatigue and sleep deprivation put a damper on your sex drive, but they can also be damaging to your overall health. If you fear that you may be walking around in a chronically foggy state of sleep deprivation (and, therefore, sex deprivation!), here are some handy tips to help alleviate the problem:

◆ **Establish a sleep routine.** Try to go to bed at roughly the same time and get up at roughly the same time every day. Also, if you like to listen to soft music or drink decaffeinated tea before bed, these activities could become part of your bedtime routine.

♦ **Avoid caffeine at night.** Stimulating substances such as caffeine can keep you up way past your bedtime.

♦ **Your bed is for sex *and* for sleep.** If you read, watch television, or use your laptop computer in bed, you may be associating bedtime with activities that have nothing to do with your bed's two primary functions: making love and sleeping.

♦ **Dim the Lights.** Consider using dimmer switches in the bedroom, because lighting that is too bright can be distracting (and not terribly romantic) when the two of you want to make love or go to sleep.

♦ **Lovemaking is the best night-time exercise.** Avoid regular exercise before bedtime, because it boosts your energy level, which is not ideal for sleep preparation. But, lovemaking is the one all-important exception to this rule, because after you make love, you feel deeply relaxed and ready for sleep!

♦ **Turn insomnia into sex.** If you can't sleep, make good use of your insomnia by making love. After all, it's much more satisfyingly than taking a sleeping pill!

♦ **Keep cool temperatures.** Be sure to keep your bedroom temperature at a comfortable level. Many people think that cooler works best for lovemaking and sleep. Maybe this is the case, because when you feel a little chilly, it's nice to snuggle together and make love to stay warm!

♦ **Limit alcohol consumption.** Try to avoid drinking alcohol close to bedtime. While drinking can sometimes make you fall asleep faster, it can also cause you to wake up more frequently during the night.

♦ **White noise can be relaxing.** Some people find they can sleep more soundly if they have "white noise" in the background. A humidifier or fan usually serves this purpose well. Also, white noise can make you feel more confident about vocalizing your pleasure during your lovemaking, because it is great for blocking out noise if there are children or houseguests in your home.

◆ **Consult your partner and your doctor.** Pay attention if your partner tells you that you have been snoring a lot, sleeping restlessly, or pausing for several seconds between breaths during sleep. You may want to ask your doctor to refer you for a sleep evaluation to determine whether you have *sleep apnea* or some other sleep disorder.

def•i•ni•tion

Sleep apnea is a condition in which a person stops breathing during sleep, sometimes hundreds of times on a given night, and sometimes for a full minute or even longer. If you think you or your partner may be suffering from sleep apnea, please consult your physician.

Your Personal Space

Solitude, alone time, and personal space are all terms to describe that time you spend by yourself to restore your supply of emotional and sexual energy. People find solitude in different ways. Some create a stress-free space or room of their own in their homes that serves as a personal haven. Others find solitude in a community setting, people-watching, or just getting lost in a crowd, while others find it in an artists' colony or spiritual facility. Still others seek out nature, the wilderness.

As a matter of fact, there are some couples who sometimes sleep in separate bedrooms, not out of lack of interest or conflict, but just to gain some personal space while both partners are in the house. By having their occasional alone nights, they find that they long to get back under the sheets together the following night or morning, and sometimes even the same night!

All are searching for time and space for contemplative and meditative thinking, whether for religious purposes, soul-searching, or simply ponder the profound sense of gratitude they feel for their lives, partners, family, and friends. To top it all off, finding time and space for solitude is a fantastic way to tune into your senses and enhance your sexual desire. After all, people who periodically grant themselves the gift of thoughtful solitude often return to their partners feeling refreshed, recharged, and ready to plunge back into all aspects of their busy lives—including making love with their partners—with renewed vigor, stamina, and joy.

The Least You Need to Know

◆ When you feel attractive, healthy, strong, and you have a positive body image, you are more inclined to experience an enhanced level of sexual desire.

◆ Learning how to engage in positive self-talk, as opposed to negative self-talk, is a key way to increase your self-esteem and your sexual desire.

◆ The images we see in the media of perfect faces and perfect bodies are quite literally not to be believed; it's not constructive to compare yourself in any way to these false images.

◆ Becoming mindful of healthy, sensual eating can make you more aware of the needs of your senses, including your sexual desire.

◆ Getting enough sleep, exercise, and alone time are all important factors in staying healthy and boosting your sexual desire.

Part 3

Prioritizing Your Relationship

You and your partner are both very busy people with many commitments and obligations. Children, careers, and life's never-ending and ever-changing list of responsibilities often leave little time or energy for your relationship with your partner.

The chapters in this next section of the book focus on understanding the different areas of your life that need and require your time and attention—your couple relationship, your family, and your work—and how to achieve a healthy balance between them all. You'll find creative, practical tips and strategies for making your relationship with your partner one of your absolute top priorities and your sexual desire soar to new heights.

Couple Time

In This Chapter

◆ Understanding couple time and its importance for sexual desire

◆ How to keep couple time a priority and stay connected with your partner

◆ Practical ways to create desire-enhancing couple time

◆ The value of planned and spontaneous date nights

Remember when you were falling in love? You couldn't wait to see each other. You couldn't wait to be alone, to hold his hand, to kiss and cuddle. Remember how exciting and electrifying it felt to touch and brush up against each other?

Well, even if the two of you have been together for years, and have lost some of that "lovin' feeling," you can, with awareness and determination, recapture those wonderful feelings from the early days of your romance. All it takes is some reflection and a slight shifting around of your priorities.

What Is Couple Time and Why You Need It

Couple time can't be overestimated or taken for granted. It's not just the hour or two alone that the two of you have at the end of the day, when everyone else in the house has gone to bed. Couple time consists of special connections, intimate moments, lift-your-spirits phone calls, and sexy, knowing glances the two of you share, as well as the time you make for and devote to each other.

In everyone there is a tremendous longing to sustain the euphoric feelings of new romance, to connect with your partner, enhance your bonds, and grow together. Couple time enables you to strengthen and further explore the behaviors, attitudes, and loving practices that sustain your connection.

Don't Let Life Get in the Way

The combined pressures of careers, kids, aging parents, volunteer activities, hobbies, and everything else you do can easily push kissing, cuddling, and making love with your partner to the back burner. These pressures that can interfere with your love life can even cause it to stall. If your relationship has fallen into a pattern absent of sexual connection, both emotional and physical, you need couple time to reclaim this essential relationship bond. Making just a handful of minor lifestyle changes can reduce your stress level, increase your energy level, and give you more time and energy, and desire, to devote to your relationship. Things like slipping loving gestures and words into your day and making more time and space for yourselves as a couple are lifestyle adjustments and changes that can jumpstart a stalled love life.

Be More Than Just Ships Passing in the Night

When you are both always running off in opposite directions, it can be a struggle to get "face time" with each other. Phone conversations and e-mail exchanges are just not the same as being in each other's presence.

Maybe you work days and he works nights. Or maybe he has a boss who requires him to put in 60—70 hours per week at the office, leaving you to fend for yourself with the kids at home. Or perhaps your job requires you to travel several times a year, forcing him to hold down the fort while you are out of town.

Or maybe your work schedules are generally in sync, but other activities (a child's soccer practice or your PTO meetings) are eating into time that you could be spending together. When it comes to living your day-to-day lives as a couple, to be and stay connected you need to be able to see each other, hold each other, and talk to each other for more than a minute at a time here and there.

And you must have time for making love. And by time, of course, we don't mean just the time required for engaging in the act itself. You also need time to switch gears, set the mood, and engage in as much foreplay as you'd like. And then after sex, you both need time to relax, drink in the experience, and bask in the afterglow.

When the two of you make time in your busy schedules for each other—and specifically when you make time for sex—you are sending each other the message that your relationship is important, most important, among all the other demands you both face, and that it's as important now as it was when you first met.

When the majority of your conversations with each other last no longer than a couple of minutes, and revolve around purely practical issues (like who needs to be where and at what time), something has got to change. It's not that your other roles and happenings in life (parenting, keeping house, working outside the home, etc.) are not important. They are. It's just that your roles as lovers are also just as, if not more, important.

But often it's these key roles—your role as your partner's lover, and her role as yours—that get shortchanged, as if your relationship can simply be taken for granted because it will always be there.

The problem, however, with taking each other (and your sex life) for granted is that intimate love relationships require tenderness, nurturing, and care if they are to thrive. Think about it like this: you would never dream of ignoring your children or not satisfying their needs for love, attention, food, shelter, clothing, etc. So if the bulk of your couple time consists of 1-minute chats here or 30-second exchanges there, you are probably not putting enough time (or effort) into your relationship.

Speaking of making an effort, some relationships just float along with-out much conflict—but without much romance, spice, or excitement, either. Often, the two partners have gotten stuck in the rut of just existing rather than living every aspect of their lives (including their sexual relationship) to the fullest.

Getting your love life on track will require both of you to ask about—and then work on meeting—each other's needs and desires, inside and outside of the bedroom. You should both voice your wishes as clearly and directly as possible so that you can each fulfill each other's desires.

How to Get and Stay Connected

True romance and couple time come down to making sure that you and your partner are connected, continuously connecting and enjoying your time together. Here are ways to make your relationship a top priority that will enhance your sexual desire.

Keep In Touch

There are several opportunities and little ways throughout the day for couples to keep in touch in purely a relationship-connecting sort of way. Put a love note in his jacket or write a loving message on the bathroom mirror with soap. Instead of just exchanging information about schedules and to-do lists, inject little expressions of love into your everyday communications, like adding some Xs and Os, drawing some lips or a heart, or coming up with your own words or symbols that sig-nal to each other your special connection.

A sexy glance, a flirtatious wink or smile, a little nibble on the ear—none of these things take a lot of time, but they sure do make your con-nection happier and sweeter and more exciting! Sexual passion builds on itself, one tiny gesture at a time.

Greet each other with a smile and kisses at the beginning and end of each day, and be sure to give each other three full-body hugs per day.

Couple time can run the gamut from a 2-minute check-in at the breakfast table when pressed for time, to intimate pillow talk at the end of the day, to a weekend away just to be together. It's about creating opportunities for intimacy wherever you are and whatever you are doing—a walk in the park or a jump in the shower together or even a quick getaway to the motel across town (why not?). Couple time is an everyday essential that gives both of you time and energy to deal with life's pressures and demands.

Get Back in the Sex Habit

If the two of you have gotten out of the habit of having as much sex as you would like, you may feel a bit rusty, anxious, and even slightly intimidated about gearing up to try again. But as daunting as this prospect can be, it is important to try to rekindle the flame.

A couple can fall out of the sex habit for any number of reasons, including radically conflicting schedules, chronic fatigue (on the part of one or both partners), temporary lapses in communication, or even excessive arguing, just to name a few.

But the good news is that once the two of you are routinely setting aside enough couple time to tackle and overcome any issues you may be experiencing in your relationship, you will probably find that getting back into the sex habit is a lot like … you guessed it … riding a bike.

And as rusty as you may feel, your body actually remembers more than you may realize. So try not to worry too much, because worrying a lot is definitely *not* a good way to enhance your sexual desire.

Rather than worrying, like the famous Nike slogan says, "Just Do It!" If you and your partner decide together you need to get your sex life back on track, then it really is just a matter of getting into bed and reacquainting yourselves with the various contours—and desires—of each other's bodies. And remember it can also be great to tell each other: "I've missed you so much. I've missed making love with you. I cherish our sex life, and I want make love more often from now on."

Accentuate the Positive

Remember always that tender, loving, nurturing words rather than harsh, negative ones are the building blocks of a lasting love relationship. It's important to squeeze snippets of positive talk, both to your partner and to yourself, in between your various tasks.

Relationship expert John Gottman maintains that there is a magic ratio of positive to negative comments in a relationship. If you pay your significant other *five* compliments in the course of a day and make only *one* negative comment, your relationship has a better chance to survive and grow than if you are constantly nit-picking at each other.

def•i•ni•tion

Psychological reframing involves, for example, deliberately choosing to view couple time in a different—and usually more positive—light.

Sometimes it can be easy to get overwhelmed by negative emotions and caught up in what you haven't accomplished on a given day. But there is a handy psychological trick for dealing with this kind of worry: it's called reframing, or, more precisely, *psychological reframing.*

If necessary, you may want to do a little reframing to bring a more positive attitude into your bedroom with your partner. For instance, instead of thinking of couple time as just another duty to be added to your already-lengthy list of chores, think of it as the most satisfying part of your day. Instead of thinking, "I don't have enough time with my partner," think, "I always have time for my partner."

Love Booster

Phrases like "I always have time for my partner" and "Our time together is always quality" are ways to accentuate the positive in your relationship.

In other words, you have the power to view your couple time in a positive, optimistic light, if you choose to exercise this power. Taking a positive approach to your time together fills you with the sort of "can do" attitude that will make all aspects of your life (including your romantic life) more fulfilling and joyous.

Having a positive outlook will work wonders for your sex life because it will help you approach your lovemaking with renewed gusto and enthusiasm. And, your renewed zest for life will help ignite your flames of passion.

Not only that, positive energy is contagious! Your reinvigorated attitude toward romance (and life in general) is bound to rub off on your partner, who will likely become excited by your excitement.

Simplify and "Sexify" Your Lives

A big part of paring down your week to create more time and space for couple time involves designing a schedule that includes making love and hanging out together. With that in mind, here are some specific ways to get sex and each other into your days.

Pare Down to Pair Up

Enhancing your sexual passion is not just about learning new techniques or positions in bed; it's also about learning how not to burn yourself out physically and emotionally before you even reach the bedroom. Bearing that in mind, ask yourself whether all of your daily activities are truly necessary; then prioritize them and determine if one or more of them could be eliminated without too much pain.

Saying no to excessive outside demands enables you to spend more time saying "Yes!" to one another. You are committed to each other for many reasons, and one of those reasons is lovemaking! Remember that you are not obligated to accept every social or professional invitation that comes your way.

Even freeing up just 1 hour a day can make you both feel liberated and ready for love. And if you do manage to free up that 1 hour, don't fill it up with another activity. Set it aside as couple time that you can spend connecting—talking, laughing, and making love.

On a related note, if you currently have any toxic, negative, cruel, or even just plain old energy-sucking people in your life, try not to spend any more of your valuable time with them than may be absolutely necessary. Paring down on these relationships that cause

> **Mood Killer**
>
> Filling all your time with activities separate from your partner and hanging out with negative people can only hinder your relationship and attitude.

you stress or drag you down will benefit your emotional health and enable you to focus that precious time and energy instead on creating more couple time with your partner.

Housework Never Felt This Good!

There are ways to turn the more mundane responsibilities of life into sexy together time. For instance, be playful and sexy with household chores, like making the beds just to mess them up again or cooking dinner together as a form of foreplay of what's to come later.

Washing the car together can be especially sexy, what with all that water and soap and wet clothing, especially if you and your mate are telling each other what you want to do in bed. Or why not get a little hot with each other while going through the automatic car wash? When it comes to flirting and making love with your partner, there is no time quite like the present, so get busy!

Relax Together for Better Sex

Instead of pushing yourselves so hard all the time to complete all the projects on your never-ending to do list, give yourselves a break and try taking things a little slower. Notice how much sexier you feel when you are both deeply relaxed. Couples who make a point of relaxing together make love more often than those who work non-stop.

In fact, many sex and medical experts have discovered that there is a powerful connection between being in a calm, relaxed state of mind and having more rewarding sex life. After all, how can you experience pleasure (sexual or otherwise) if you are in a tense, wound-up state of mind? So turn a portion of your couple time into a session of just relaxing together ... and that can set the stage for sex.

One sexy way to relax together is to stretch together (perhaps in the nude, if you think that might be fun). Or you may want to take a warm bath together, or try breathing deeply together perhaps with meditation, which can not only be relaxing, but can also create a strong emotional bond.

Notable Quotable

"How to have good sex: relax, relax, relax."

—Jay Schlechter, Ph.D., Author of *Intimate Friends*

You can't feel relaxed, limber, and ready for lovemaking if you are holding your breath or your muscles feel clenched up and tight. Great sex and relaxed bodies go together.

Love Booster

"Breathing can have a tremendous effect on sex. The more complete the breathing, the deeper the experience of sex. That's why some people say that relaxed and easy breathing is the gateway to sexual ease."

—William Ashoka Ross

Be Fully Present

When you spend time with your partner, make sure you are totally engaged with and "present" to each other. Don't let your thoughts race around in a million directions. After a hectic day, it can sometimes be hard to quiet and simplify your mind, but it's important to try, for the sake of enhancing your sex life.

To quiet your mind during intimate moments, focus solely on your partner, her touch, the sound of her voice, the loving look in her eyes, and the feel of her skin. People (especially the people who know you the best) quickly sense when your thoughts are elsewhere, which can be hurtful. So use these sensory tools to be fully present, alert, and in the moment when you are getting intimate with your partner.

Make Your Bedroom Your Getaway

Think of your bedroom as your romantic getaway. It can happen when you have children that the entire house gets devoted to the kids and filled to the brim with their games and toys. But remember there should be one exception, one space in the house that is reserved just for you and your partner—your master bedroom and, if possible, bathroom. Make your bedroom a master suite beautifully and romantically decorated to resemble a honeymoon suite in one of the finest hotels. Make it a private sanctuary where you can escape to make love or just get away from the everyday hectic pace.

You don't need a big home-decorating budget, but you may want to take a few steps to make your bedroom as cozy and intimate as possible. Buying a plush bedspread or changing your current lighting to make it softer and more inviting and romantic could do the trick. Or try painting the walls a fresh color, which is something you could do as a form of couple time.

The point is not to spend hours and thousands of dollars on redecorating your bedroom. Rather, the point is that your bedroom is the intimate space that you share with your partner. The two of you deserve to have this space arranged in a romantic way that suits your tastes and gets you both in the mood for love.

Turn Off the Phone, and Turn On the Passion

There are certain times of day when turning off your cell phone, your fax machine, and your computer can have big benefits. If you're too busy working online or just surfing the net, you may not notice that your partner is standing by waiting to get close to you. And even if you are just going to watch television together, just being on the couch together and cuddling after a long day can be more important than taking a phone call that might tie you up unnecessarily for 20 minutes or longer.

Cell phones, in particular, are a big source of distraction in this day and age. Send a clear signal to your partner that he is the most important person to you, especially during couple time, by ignoring phone calls and even saying out loud "Whoever it is can wait."

No matter what you're doing together—having a casual conversation, watching a movie, or heading to the bedroom—ignoring distractions like the phone can really serve to ignite the passion.

Sexy Ways to Shift Gears and Decompress

At the end of the day, you may wish to change from your work clothes into something more comfortable. But remember that comfortable doesn't have to mean dowdy or unflattering. Comfortable should also mean sexy, soft, and sensuous. Make sure you smell good with a few quick sprits of perfume. Brush your teeth and rub on some fragrant lotion to feel refreshed, sensual, and ready for making love.

When you want to shift gears from work mode to love mode, give yourself and your partner plenty of time and space to decompress. Unwinding or decompressing can mean different things to different people. Maybe you like to sit quietly in your favorite comfortable chair for a few minutes before preparing dinner, or perhaps you like to exercise or listen to soft music.

Decompression time helps you relax, and when you're relaxed and less stressed, you are more likely to get in the mood for making love. So figure out which decompression techniques work best for you, both as individuals and as a couple.

Of course, you probably won't be able to go through an elaborate decompression ritual every single evening. But it's a good idea to at least try for some decompression time together every once in a while. Whenever you can, the two of you may want to have a glass of wine with cheese and crackers while listening to some soft, sexy music together.

If the weather is good, take a stroll outside, or if you have a fireplace, make a fire and relax in front of it. In terms of couple time, there may be nothing quite as relaxing and romantic as watching flames flickering in a hearth.

Try to incorporate sexiness into your decompression routine. Remember, couple time can be spent in the form of down time, unwinding from a long day, and it can be used as a time to express and enhance your sexual desire.

When Couple Time Turns into Family Time

For couples with children, some couple time inevitably morphs into family time. After all, you can't schedule scraped knees or any of the other unexpected situations that can arise when you have children. But keep in mind when this happens that it's not the end of the world (we'll address family time in greater detail in Chapter 8).

For instance, if you have kids and they are home needing your attention when the two of you are trying to have some time together decompressing and relaxing, you will probably need to incorporate them into part or all of this time. But don't despair; get creative instead!

If you like to sit in the backyard and watch the sunset together, engage the kids in activities they can play outside so the two of you can watch them and the sunset at the same time. You can be together as a couple (your own unit of two sitting on the porch) and together as a family (the two of you watching the kids play), all at the same time.

In other words, family time can sometimes be another form of couple time—albeit a more *crowded* form. Granted, it is not as intimate as one-on-one couple time, but it is valuable for your relationship as a couple in a different way. When you are with your whole family, your primary focus obviously is not on your intimate relationship with your partner. That's okay as long as you also manage to squeeze in some private time, too.

One reason that family time can actually be good for your relationship is that anything that enhances your emotional bond as a couple (including fun, well-spent family time) has the potential to enhance your sexual bond as well … as soon as the two of you can actually get a little privacy, that is!

It's a Date!

Dates aren't just for singles and courting couples. Going out with your partner for date nights—treating yourselves to exclusive time and experiences together—is a very important component of couple time.

Is it a good idea to schedule date nights, or is spontaneity more fun? When you have children, scheduling is typically mandatory, but it also gives you something to look forward to, and gives you that wonderful sensation of anticipation. On the other hand, spontaneity can certainly be exciting as well, so when your in-laws offer to take the kids for the night at the last minute, take full advantage of it!

And remember, weekends are for fun! So, as often as possible, keep your weekends as free and clear as you can so that you can set aside at least some of that time for intimate activity with your partner.

If your weekends are almost as packed with activities as your weekdays, you may need to pare down to the bare essentials with your weekend schedule; create more time and space for making love and hanging out together as a couple.

Scheduling Date Nights

If you take the time to pencil the words "date night" into your daily planner, it is more likely you will follow through with the plan. Also, whenever you see those words next to the other appointments in your calendar, you will be reminded that you are putting balance into your schedule, making time for you and your partner, and that your life has much more to it than just boring, necessary appointments.

There is real value to scheduling dates and times to be intimate, because anticipating lovemaking with your partner can be almost as exciting as the sex itself.

You can use your date nights to talk about how you are doing as a couple, that is, to conduct a sort of weekly or bi-weekly "state of the relationship" conversation. If there is a specific issue going on in your relationship that needs to be addressed—a communication block, for example—you may want to schedule a date night to work through the problem in order to rekindle the flame.

Love Booster

"People tend to wait for the perfect mood to strike or the right moment to arrive, because they fear that anything planned will cheapen the experience and make it artificial, but anticipation could be a powerful aphrodisiac."

—Mark Michaels and Patricia Johnson, Authors of *The Essence of Tantric Sexuality*

Spontaneous Date Nights

If the two of you find the idea of planning a date night too regimented or formal, try to think of any private time you have together as potential opportunities for making love. Spontaneous date nights are occasions for fun and romance. When you sweep your mate off his feet and surprise him with a reservation at his favorite restaurant, or tickets to a game, or even a romantic dinner at home, it can only lead to good times.

Spontaneous dates can shake up your routine, pull you out of your ordinary lives, and bring back a sense of excitement and newness to your relationship. If there is something you both have been dying to try—rock-climbing, for instance—then why not surprise your partner with a day trip somewhere for an afternoon of rock-climbing?

How You Like It

Whether the two of you prefer your date nights for being playful and lighthearted or for engaging in deep, meaningful conversations, know that either of these can increase your feelings of emotional intimacy—which means they can also enhance your sexual desire for each other. If you decide to go out to dinner, consider choosing a restaurant that is totally different from the unromantic, family-oriented places that you may go to with your kids. Your date nights should really feel special and be a break from the ordinary, so be sure to pick a place you wouldn't necessarily go to with the whole family, whether it's quiet with soft lights and romantic ambiance or noisy with a bar and live band.

Love Booster

When it comes to date night, it's fun and sexy to get dressed up—wear something you don't wear everyday and you'll turn both of you on.

And once you are there, don't be shy about getting romantic, no matter what the setting. Date nights are about reconnecting and recapturing the romance and sensuality of your early courting days. So hold hands and be sure to steal a few kisses. Think of these sexy gestures as pre-bedroom foreplay.

Getting a Babysitter

We'll talk extensively about the children dynamic in the next chapter, but it's worth mentioning here that it's healthy, and essential, if you have children to occasionally get a trusted babysitter to watch your children for a few hours or even overnight so you and your partner can have some alone couple time.

The two of could get a hotel room for the night and add yet another layer of excitement to your date night. When you go to a hotel instead of staying home, you are sending each other the message that this is a special night, a break from your ordinary routine, which is wonderful for enhancing your mutual sexual desire.

Or, send the children to their grandparents' or friends' house so that you can have a private date night at home. After all, you may be happier and more comfortable staying in, rather than heading out for a night on the town. You can make dinner and watch a movie, or head straight up to the bedroom for some extended intimate time.

Doing Couple Hobbies and Activities Together

Couple time is also about enjoying hobbies together, whether they are of interest to both or just one of you. Use daily activities, date nights, and opportunities to get a babysitter to discover and experience hobbies and activities the two of you enjoy.

For instance, if you love to garden, it can be lot of fun to do this together. For starters, just feeling the soil running through your fingers can be a sensual experience. And of course, talking and laughing together in the relaxed setting of your own yard can strongly enhance your closeness and your sense of emotional connectedness and intimacy.

Or in another example, your partner may play golf, yet you don't know how. You can take an afternoon to go out play together and have the sexy, sensual experience of your partner showing you how to swing and putt. In turn, you can take him out and show him something you like to do. Participating with each other in activities you enjoy, whatever they are, strengthens your feelings of emotional intimacy with your partner, and this can strongly enhance your sexual desire.

The Least You Need to Know

- ◆ Couple time is any intimate quality time spent with your partner during the day, from a loving 2-minute check-in at breakfast to making love at the end of your day.

- ◆ Don't let hectic schedules prevent you from having enough couple time; shift your schedule around to have more face time with your partner.

◆ Staying connected as a couple involves finding creative ways to keep in touch during your busy days, getting back into the sex habit (if you have fallen out of it), and accentuating the positive.

◆ Relaxing together and paring down your schedules can lead to more satisfying sex, and being more sexually and emotionally available to each other.

◆ Planned and spontaneous date nights with your partner help boost sexual desire and enhance your life.

Chapter 8

Family Time

In This Chapter

- ◆ How to balance family time and couple time
- ◆ Different stages of child development that present different opportunities and challenges for couples
- ◆ Desire-enhancing aspects of becoming new parents
- ◆ Necessary lifestyle and sex-life adjustments once kids enter the picture

In this chapter, we will talk about ways to blend and harmonize your family time with your couple time. We don't have to tell you that there are only 24 hours in a day. You spend 7 or 8 of those hours sleeping, and another 8 (often more) working. Your daily schedule can leave you with little time, or energy, to spend with the people you love most in the world, as well as for making love.

Naturally, your children always need you. They always need your unconditional love, attention, nurturing, encouragement, and guidance. But it's important to remember that you and your partner need that, too, to be able, in turn, to provide all those things for your children. The focus of this chapter is how to integrate meeting the needs of your family with your needs as a couple.

No Children of Your Own

Of course, parenthood is not everyone's cup of tea. Not all couples have children or plan to have children. If this is your situation, this chapter may not have a direct application to your lives.

However, if the two of you have nieces or nephews or other children who play a big role in your lives, and you in theirs, or even if you'd just like to gain an understanding and empathy for what your friends, siblings, and relatives face in the balancing act of the couple and the family, this information will be helpful and insightful to you.

Waiting to Have Children

A fair number of couples wait before having children. One of the main benefits of taking this path of waiting is that you get to spend a significant amount of uninterrupted couple time together before your family of two grows into a family of three (or four, or five, or six …). Any time you spend building your bond as a couple during this pre-family period can only serve to strengthen your feelings of sexual desire for each other. It can also strengthen your mutual sense of emotional and physical intimacy, which will help you greatly when little people enter your mix.

Specifically, if you and your partner are waiting to have kids, be sure to take advantage of this golden opportunity to relish in and nurture each other as much as you possibly can. After all, the undivided attention that you are able to lavish on each other now, during this blissfully unencumbered time in your lives, is bound to become much more limited once your children are born. This also means that your chances for spontaneous lovemaking or for making love in different rooms or in creative places—like on top of the kitchen table!—will be much harder to come by. So what are you waiting for? Put the book down and get busy!

Whether you and your partner ultimately decide to have children or not, remember that your connection as a couple is what's paramount. So no matter what, be sure to keep nurturing that precious bond. After all, it's the foundation, not only to a harmonious home and family life, but also to a continually fulfilling sex life.

Taking the Plunge

Becoming a parent is a phenomenal, joyous experience. In fact, many people would describe it as one of the best things that has ever happened to them. But it is also emotionally complicated, and can present challenges to your relationship as a couple.

Even positive life changes, such as getting married or finding a good job, can stress you out, sometimes quite profoundly. And becoming a parent certainly qualifies as a major life stressor, albeit a generally positive one.

Let's assume the decision-making is behind you, and you've made the seismic shift from couplehood to parenthood. How can you keep your sexual desire going strong throughout the challenging days and years of parenthood ahead? Some answers can be found in the way you and your partner handle the various stages of your children's development.

The Infant, Toddler, and Preschooler Years

If you have a newborn, or one or more children under the age of 3, chances are there are many days when you are just so physically tired and drained from taking care of them around the clock that the idea of working up enough energy and passion for sex with your partner is, well, to put it bluntly, almost laughable. There may be days when you feel lucky if you can find enough time to squeeze in a shower, much less sex. In fact, the only thing you crave in these days is sleep, sleep, and more sleep.

Post-Delivery Sex Drive

You may experience a natural dip in your sex drive directly following childbirth. This is normal and to be expected, and it has to do with hormones and the chronic exhaustion that comes with caring for small children.

A big part of getting your sexual appetite back once you become a parent is to educate yourself and your partner about what your body is going through after you give birth. Knowledge, as they say, is power. A temporary reduction in your sex drive is a natural part of new parenthood; it will not last forever. So give yourself and your partner permission to be gentle and compassionate with each other during this special time.

Ease your way into your post-delivery intimate life gently and with great tenderness, not only toward your partner, but also toward yourself. It's better to wait to resume making love with your partner until you are really up to it, both physically and emotionally. Only then it will be a happy, memorable experience for you both for all of the *right* reasons.

If you are craving more touch and less intercourse, say to your partner, remembering your positive talk skills: "Honey, I'm craving your touch," rather than: "Don't touch me." The latter can be extremely debilitating to resuming healthy intimacy.

Or you might want to say: "Right now I'm in the mood for touching but not intercourse. Is that okay with you?" This approach works particularly well because it's honest, direct, and clear.

Reassure him that this is a stage you are going through, and that your sexual desire will return … when the kids move out of the house—just joking! It will indeed return very soon, but it just takes a little time. And a loving, caring, *educated*, and empathic partner will understand and be patient.

For example, let's say "Linda," who is 28 years old has been married to her husband "Jim" for three years. When they first got married, like most newlyweds, they had sex quite frequently. But then Jim fell off his bike and broke four ribs and his right leg, and Linda got pregnant and gained 60 pounds during her pregnancy. After she gave birth she breastfed for four months. She also exercised, which helped her to lose 45 of the 60 pounds she had gained. But she still feels self-conscious about the remaining 15 pounds. Nor is she happy with the changes her body has gone through following childbirth and breastfeeding, changes which include a c-section scar and a few fading stretch marks on her belly and breasts.

Now their baby daughter "Ellie" is seven months old. But between Jim's leftover soreness from his old bike accident, Linda's lingering self-consciousness about her body, and their general fatigue because baby Ellie is still not sleeping through the night, neither of them has felt an enormous amount of sexual desire in the past few months.

In addition, there are many days when Linda feels she gets more than her fill of physical and emotional contact just from holding, kissing and caring for Ellie all day long. When night comes, she feels she has nothing left to give.

Whether they realize it or not, Linda and Jim are actively grieving the loss of their old pre-injury and pre-childbirth selves, as well as the loss of the unencumbered, happy-go-lucky newlywed couple they used to be not so long ago.

Some couples in this situation find it helpful to acknowledge out loud they are not the same people they were prior to becoming parents. As ecstatic as they are to have their dear baby in their lives, they sense they have lost the people they once were. The loss is genuine, and it is a loss worth mourning. As we (and many mental health professionals) often say, even the good changes that people undergo, such as becoming parents for the first time, can be stressful and fraught with complicated emotions.

This is why it's so important for both partners to be extra encouraging and supportive of each other during this time. For instance, Jim continues to tell Linda how hot and gorgeous he finds her. And Linda tells Jim how sweet and helpful he is with the baby.

These compliments and words of encouragement keep them going during their often sleepless nights. And as hard as it may be for them to believe right now, this constant flow of positive, nurturing words and gestures will help Jim and Linda gradually move beyond their soreness, fatigue and self-consciousness to a place of renewed and reinvigorated sexual desire.

Some helpful websites that regularly feature informative articles on the topic of how becoming a new mother can affect your sexual desire, here are: www.babyzone.com, www.iVillage.com www.femalepatient.com, www.SexualHealth.com and www.womenshealth.com.

Two helpful books (also included in Appendix A) explain how a woman's sex drive can ebb and flow in direct relation to her hormonal activity at any given time, including the period immediately following childbirth: *I'm Not in The Mood: What Every Woman Should Know about Improving Her Libido*, by Dr. Judith Reichman and *Okay, So I Don't Have a Headache: What I Learned (and What All Women Need to Know) about Hormones, PMS, Stress, Diet, Menopause—and Sex*, by Cristina Ferrare.

In 2005, Sandra Pertot, Ph.D., published the rather provocatively titled book, *Perfectly Normal: Living and Loving with Low Libido*. She had written her doctoral dissertation on the topic of women who lose their desire for and enjoyment of sex following childbirth.

In *Perfectly Normal*, she describes the research she conducted in the 1970s, when she was writing her dissertation. She came across a variety of competing theories as to why so many women lose their desire for sex after delivering babies. For instance, one theory popular at the time held that after a woman gives birth, she tends to view herself solely as a mother, and can no longer see herself as a sexual being. This theory was later debunked.

After conducting three studies of her own, Dr. Pertot discovered the most prevalent cause reported by new mothers who lacked sexual desire was good old-fashioned fatigue. One half of the mothers she interviewed during the course of her research stated they were still less interested in sex a full year into new motherhood than they had been prior to becoming mothers.

So, if you are a new mother, be patient and gentle with yourself. After all, as anyone who has ever cared for small children knows, as emotionally rewarding as it is, it is also one of the most difficult, physically demanding and exhausting tasks in the world. So if your sexual desire is not kicking back into high gear after the birth of your baby, please don't chastise yourself for it.

While doing her doctoral research, Dr. Pertot also discovered even though a solid 50% of the women she interviewed reported less sexual desire during the year following childbirth, only a quarter of the same group (25%) reported less sexual enjoyment. This particular finding adds credence to the ever-growing pile of evidence we mentioned in Chapter 4 in support of the theory that once people (and women in particular) with relatively low sexual desire start to engage in sexual activity, they often enjoy the experience very much.

In Dr. Pertot's opinion, couples can retrieve their old feelings of desire for and enjoyment of sex after childbirth (or after any after any other stressful life event). The key is to be patient and loving with each other, and to acknowledge and accept the fact that in any long-term relationship, the frequency of sex, as well as the desire for sex, will inevitably ebb and flow. And often there is a direct connection between this ebb and flow and big life events, such as new parenthood.

Finally, a particularly salient statistic on women and diminished sexual desire comes from a landmark 1999 American sex study published in *JAMA* in 1999. Medical scholars analyzed data from the National Health and Social Life Survey. Involving 1,749 female participants 1,410 male participants, and the study revealed that 31 percent of women between the ages of 18–59 experience low sexual desire at some point in their lives. (We will discuss some additional findings from this important study in a later section of this chapter.)

Your Affections

Having a brand new baby in the house just naturally brings out your affectionate side. You spend hours cuddling and cooing with your little one. But when you show affection to your child, remember that your partner needs some, too. New dads sometimes feel pushed aside when their partners give nearly all of their affection to their child. Because remember, before the baby came, you were giving all of that to him.

Some couples find that the hot sex they had before they had kids has morphed into just tender affection.

Sometimes dads want sex before the new moms are ready. And sometimes a new mother may not want her partner to touch her at all for fear that he will want intercourse.

This can be a challenging time in a relationship. But when you acknowledge to each other that your partnership is evolving, that your identities are shifting, you can relax in the knowledge that your relationship is moving into a new stage, and so is your lovemaking. You are no longer just partners; you are parents, too.

"If you've stopped feeling sexual because of being bitten by the motherhood bug, it's important to make a conscious decision to make your marriage a priority. I always say that the best thing you can do for your children is to put your marriage first. Take more time for your spouse." —Michele Weiner Davis, author of *The Sex-Starved Marriage: Boosting Your Marriage Libido*

Emotional Turn-Ons of New Parenthood

Everything is so new and different once you enter the world of parenthood. This newness has a very positive side that might surprise you.

For instance, many new mothers report that their partners are helping more around the house. They are making the transition to fatherhood smoothly and lovingly. Just knowing how much your partner adores you and your children can be a potent emotional turn-on. And as we've discussed, emotional turn-ons help rekindle the flame of your sexual desire.

When you experience an energizing burst of sexual desire, as long as you are feeling up to it—both emotionally and physically—you may want to initiate sex with your partner. After all, it's important for him to know that you still find him sexy and desirable. And it's fantastic for both of you to rediscover just how much fun sex can be, in case you forgot among all the baby excitement, and how much tension it can relieve!

The Elementary School Years

When your children leave their preschool years behind, you may find yourselves facing new joys and new challenges as you are all entering a new stage of life in the household. On the joyous side, you and your partner may discover that you have more time on your hands, both as individuals and as a couple. You may also find that you have more energy to devote to one another, and particularly to your intimate life as a couple.

If you and your partner conduct your work lives at home or relatively close to home, when the kids are off at school the two of you may have more chunks of time to spend together, just the two of you, during the day that you haven't had in a while. What a special, unexpected treat. Remember, as long as you have your privacy, there's nothing wrong with an afternoon quickie!

Or if one or both of you need to commute to work, figure out a way to see each other for lunch on a regular basis to be able to enjoy some time together outside the house without the kids, in your roles as adults instead of parents. Periodic e-mails, text messages, or a quick voicemail to let your partner know you're thinking of him goes a long way in maintaining a strong emotional bond.

The Preteen and Teen Years

The house is sexually charged when teenagers are around. Indeed, when your children enter their preteen and teen years, an interesting time will surely be had by one and all, as hormones bounce all over the place and mood swings abound. One minute you'll find yourself laughing with your teenagers, and the next minute they're giving you the silent treatment.

As you know, they are struggling with leaving childhood behind and moving into adulthood, both emotionally and physiologically. And as their parents, it is inevitably the two of you who are destined to take the brunt of their struggle during these years. This is as it should be, of course, but that doesn't mean it isn't sometimes difficult to cope with their moodiness and expectations. Another point to consider is that raising teenagers often brings up your own unresolved conflicts about your teenage years. For example, if your teenager is dating, while you might be happy that he or she is having this experience, at the same time you might feel sad for yourself if you missed out on going to your high school prom. To cope with such feelings, when your teenager goes out on a date or to prom, you and your partner may want to do something special and exciting for yourselves that night.

Again, any qualms you may have about your own sexuality are going to bubble to the surface with teenagers at home. For example, if you are the mother of a teenage daughter, when you see her come of age and go out on dates, you could experience a whole range of emotions such as realizing that you're not young like her anymore and those experiences no longer lie ahead of you.

Also, maybe your teenage years were hard for you, or your partner, for one reason or another, and you're frankly quite relieved to have them behind you—and don't want to relive them with your children. Or, maybe you thoroughly enjoyed that time of your life, and watching your teenage daughter get dressed up for dates makes you nostalgic. Whatever feelings surface, it's important to acknowledge them and to be aware that such emotions are totally natural, and you are perfectly entitled to feel them.

There is also the issue of sex education. How do you talk to your kids about sex? Do you leave it up to the school? Are you open about sexuality? Who talks to your son? Who talks to your daughter?

These questions will start quite a dialogue with your partner. Perhaps the two of you will be talking about sex more now than you ever have before; you'll be getting questions from your children about it, and will need to be able to talk openly and maturely about sex and dating with them. So you best be prepared as well as educated in your own sexuality before trying to help your children sort it out. One helpful book for parents on this subject is *Everything You Never Wanted Your Kids to Know About Sex (But Were Afraid They'd Ask): The Secrets to Surviving Your Child's Sexual Development from Birth to the Teens*, by Justin Richardson and Mark Schuster. This resource can help you navigate the sensitive topic of sex with your teenagers.

Also remember that for the parents of teenagers, hanging on to your sense of humor is a key component to hanging on to your sanity. Sometimes simply commiserating and joking around with your partner about how difficult it is to cope with teenagers in the house can lead to laughter ... and perhaps, when the timing is just right, to making love.

The Challenges of Teenagers

In terms of pursuing your sex life with your partner, here's the tricky part about having teenagers in the house: they know about sex, are naturally curious about it, and often stay up late at night. Any of these realities can pose interesting challenges to the two of you when you are trying to figure out the best times to make love.

Also, the two of you may also find yourselves fielding some rather interesting, perhaps entirely unanticipated, questions from your teens about your own intimate life as a couple. Just remember that the two of you are entitled to your privacy. So, if any of the questions your teenagers ask about your own sex life strike you as too invasive or personal, feel free to say so, as it's good for them to have a solid understanding of privacy and healthy boundaries. But choose your words carefully. Use kind, gentle language that doesn't make them feel embarrassed about their natural curiosity about sex.

The Pluses of Teenagers

Regarding your sex life as a couple, here's the plus side of having teenagers in the house, (and you'll be happy to know that it's a big plus): teenagers often have ultra-full lives, including extracurricular activities, such as sports or after-school jobs. They have friendships and romantic relationships that tend to keep them occupied, distracted, and, in some cases, out of the house from morning till evening.

And of course, when your teenagers are out of the house living their own busy lives, the two of you have a golden opportunity to reconnect with each other and get intimate.

Teenagers also bring life and energy into a household. They are in transition, standing on the threshold between childhood and adulthood, and there is a lot of electricity and energy that naturally goes along with this stage of life.

For instance, teenagers love to talk (when they're in a "talking mood," that is), about what's hip, what's happening, what's going on in popular culture right now. And it can be fun and invigorating for you and your spouse to take part in these conversations. Indeed, sometimes that fresh new energy that teenagers bring into a household can help their parents feel recharged and re-energized as a couple.

The Empty-Nest Years

When your children grow up and leave home to strike out on their own, you and your partner will experience a variety of emotions. On the one hand, you will miss them very much. But on the other hand, part of you might feel downright exhilarated about being able to focus your emotional energy on your relationship as a couple.

Menopause Myths

The empty-nest years and menopause often coincide. Until quite recently, menopause was mistakenly viewed by some as a sort of death. More precisely, some viewed it as the death of a woman's sexual desire, and perhaps her entire sex life.

Fortunately, these outdated myths about menopause are disappearing. There is no need for a woman's sex life to stop when she reaches menopause. In fact, for many women and their partners this particular life passage can mark a period of sexual liberation. No more worrying about birth control ever again! Indeed, for many women, menopause is a time of life when they experience a sexual reawakening.

def•i•ni•tion

> **Perimenopause** is the phase that all women experience as they transition from having monthly periods to having no periods at all (menopause). This phase can take up to ten years.

In the landmark 1999 sex study cited earlier in this chapter, researchers discovered that 31 percent of women between the ages of 18–59 report low sexual desire; 64 percent of the women who report being affected by low sexual desire are under the age of 39. Note the majority is well under menopause age!

This same study also found that 30 percent of 30-year-old women report low sexual desire. That percentage rises to about 50 percent for women at the age of 50. Interestingly, however, and particularly relevant here, among women between the ages of 51-59, the percentage with low sexual desire drops to 27 percent! Researchers attribute this sharp decline in part to the fact postmenopausal women continue to produce androgens, which are known to enhance sexual desire.

What more proof could anyone need than the old "no sex after meno-pause" myth is a lie? It is also deeply destructive to women and their sense of themselves as fully sexual beings. (Treatment options for menopausal women who experience a decrease in sexual desire can be found in Appendix B.)

More Time For What You Want

Because menopause often overlaps with empty-nest syndrome, the two of you can finally shift the bulk of your attention away from your kids and onto each other. Just think: along with not having to worry about birth control ever again, there's also no possibility of having a kid barging in on you during lovemaking anymore. Here it's important to remember you are entering yet another phase of life, and you may need to learn and even relearn ways for connecting being sexual in this new life stage.

And as an extra bonus, if you add retirement into the mix—or at least the possibility of retiring within the next few years after the kids are on their own—your couple time will increase exponentially. And of course, having more precious couple time with your partner can only enhance your sexual desire.

Also, for both women and men, empty nest years can be wonder-ful time in life to express their full autonomy and individuation. For instance, people in their fifties often become involved in volunteer work, political activism or even decide to pursue new careers.

One somewhat controversial desire-enhancing book that addresses this particular topic is *Mating in Captivity: Reconciling the Erotic and the Domestic*, by sex therapist Esther Perel. Perel maintains (somewhat controversially) that excessive amounts of the wonderful goals most people seek in a marriage or long-term monogamous relationship, such as security, near-constant togetherness, stability, companionship, "nest-ing," etc., can sometimes be the culprits that kill sexual desire.

She believes that over time, the comforts and cozy pleasures of domes-ticity may ultimately be responsible for extinguishing the fires of sexual desire. Furthermore, she contends that to keep eroticism alive and well, couples need to find ways to infuse (or re-infuse) their sex lives with a sense of risk, naughtiness, adventure, variety and unpredictability.

You may recall that in Chapter 1 we discussed the stages of relationships. One of the later stages involves healthy "individuation." Taking that idea one step further, Ms. Perel maintains that autonomy within marriage (or any committed relationship) also happens to be one of the keys to revitalizing marital eroticism. Specifically, she believes people who have rich, fulfilling lives as individuals (in their professions, friendships, hobbies, etc.) are most likely to have exciting erotic relationships with their partners as well.

By definition, autonomous individuals don't rely on anyone other than themselves to feel whole or complete. Or, to put it another way, autonomous individuals don't believe their partners must satisfy *all* of their needs. They are not overly or unhealthily "enmeshed" with their partners. You may recall our discussion in Chapter 6 about how sexy and alluring confidence can be, particularly when that confidence comes from within, from one's own feelings of accomplishment and self-worth, rather than from external sources.

In Ms. Perel's opinion, when couples are not overly enmeshed with each other, each individual partner retains an air of mystery or "otherness" to their spouse, as opposed to an excessive degree of familiarity or domesticity. Indeed, Ms. Perel believes that autonomy—and the slight hint of mystery that comes along with it—is often exactly what's needed to boost sexual desire and keep a couple's sex life exciting.

It's not that Ms. Perel is not in favor of what we like to call couple time. She just thinks that individual time is equally important, and the pursuit of autonomy is one of the best tools couples have at their disposal to enhance their couple time and their sexual desire for one another. But you certainly don't have to wait until you're through menopause, an empty nester or retired to live to your fullest and most desired potential—do it now and reap the rewards of sexual satisfaction with your partner!

Pleasant Surprises

Some people regard the empty-nest stage of life as a time for balancing the sexual scales between men and women. Since it has often been assumed that young men want sex more frequently than young women, as some men age, they discover that they don't have to make love as frequently as they did in their younger years to feel satisfied and fulfilled.

Interestingly, and perhaps a bit ironically as well, some menopausal women experience an increase in their level of sexual desire. So that higher desire for sex that comes earlier for men, just comes later for women. Sometimes this resurgence is prompted by hormonal therapy, such as low-dose testosterone treatment (which we will discuss in greater detail in Appendix B).

But important life changes, such as the kids moving out of the house, can also prompt this resurgence. In fact, some menopausal women tell their doctors of experiencing such a strong increase in their sexual desire that their partners may actually have trouble keeping up with them in the bedroom!

Moreover, middle-aged and older men may take longer to orgasm, which means that their lovemaking lasts longer. Extended lovemaking may be of particular benefit to women, since many women find it easier to climax when lovemaking lasts longer. Prolonged lovemaking can also lead to even deeper feelings of emotional and physical intimacy between two partners.

As always, kissing, touching, hugging, and cuddling are as important for couples during the empty-nest years as they are at any other stage of life. Not only do these activities enable couples to feel close and connected, but they also help both partners maintain their confidence and sense of worth in their mature years.

A Loving Family Home

Of course, one of the best examples you can set for your children is to treat your partner with kindness. Children thrive in an atmosphere of appreciation and encouragement. So does your partner; and so do you. Notice the efforts he is making to be a good parent. Tell your partner what you appreciate about him as a father.

And at the same time, be sure to acknowledge yourself as a mother.

Share with each other what you are learning, what is hard for you, what is easy, what you like about parenting, what you need help with, etc. You both are learning, and as happens with learning any new skill, you will need encouragement from each other.

Love Booster _____

Every time you and your partner behave in a kind, warm, loving, playful way in front of your children, you are not only deepening your emotional bond with each other, but you are also demonstrating to your children what an affectionate marriage looks like.

Give each other lots of gentle, encouraging hugs. Ask for a hug or a kiss if you need it. This is the essence of good couple time. And your intimate bond as a couple is built on these small, loving gestures.

For instance, Alice adores watching her husband Craig smile and hold the baby; and she tells him so often. Craig tenderly kisses the baby's cheeks and walks the baby when Alice needs sleep. And although he struggled with becoming comfortable changing diapers and giving the baby a bath, he has slowly gotten the hang of it.

The efforts Craig makes touch Alice's heart, and she says so. Instead of taking his efforts for granted, she acknowledges with her words and her actions just how much his love gestures mean to her. She slips her hand into his, touches his knee, gives him a kiss, and says, "Thank you for being such a good father."

In these intimate moments, they come together not only as parents, but also as a couple, fully committed to each other and fully committed to being good parents. This tender acknowledgment creates a family circle, a bond that will get all of them through the pressures of daily life.

Promising Research on Arousal

If you have only recently become a parent, believe it or not, the time really will come when you feel like moving beyond just kissing and touching, and you will genuinely want to get back to having sexual intercourse with your partner.

Fortunately, according to many sex and relationship experts, studies show that *you* have the power to get yourself in the mood, even when you are feeling spent or distracted. Sometimes the key to re-igniting your sexual desire is just to get the ball rolling by kissing, cuddling, and caressing each other. This physical stimulation can relax and excite you, arouse your senses, and lead to a substantial upsurge in your sexual desire.

Indeed, the latest scientific research about human sexuality indicates that the human sexual-response cycle is not as fixed as was once believed. Previously, experts thought that the cycle *always* progressed in the following order: desire, arousal, orgasm, then satisfaction. Now we know that the cycle can have a different sequence of arousal, desire, orgasm, then satisfaction.

In other words, sometimes a woman may not have sexual thoughts or desire at the outset of a sexual encounter with her partner. Nonetheless, as soon as the two of them start to engage in stimulating sex play, this mutually arousing behavior can trigger her sexual desire, which can lead, in turn, to orgasm and a feeling of total and complete emotional and sexual satisfaction.

Keep Communication Heartfelt

Good, heartfelt communication with your partner is essential to resuming a fulfilling sex life after you have had a baby. A new mother may want to make a point of talking to her partner about how she feels, rather than allowing her innermost post-partum anxieties about sex or any other subject to remain a mystery to him. If she does this, she is bound to make significant strides.

Once you both get a chance to get all of your feelings about becoming parents out in the open, you will probably feel relaxed and unburdened, which is the ideal mindset to be in when you are preparing to make love.

Flexibility Is Key

In the child-rearing stage of life, adaptability and being willing to compromise are more important than ever. You certainly have the ability to shift smoothly from being nonparents to being parents, and to maintain and keep building upon your intimate bond as a couple. But adapting yourself to any new situation will require effort, time, and patience.

Flexibility is important when children come into the picture because you never know what's going to happen next. Let's say you have a day all planned out, right down to the minute. But then little Jack decides it might be fun to "fly" from the couch to the coffee table, badly spraining his right index finger in the process. He's crying. You're crying.

And of course, the rest of your lives get put on hold while you take him to the emergency room, where the two of you sit in the waiting room for hours. All your plans for the day, including your planned date night with your partner, go straight out the window. This doesn't mean after poor little Jack is feeling better, the two of you can't plan another night out. It just means you both need to remain flexible and ready to adapt to new developments at all times.

> **Mood Killer**
>
> Partners who are rigid, unyielding, unwilling to compromise and unable to go with the flow are more likely to disturb the delicate emotional balance in their relationships with their mates, children, loved ones and friends.

Fortunately, as we have discussed, you can achieve emotional and physical intimacy in many different, equally satisfying ways. If on a given evening you are both too tired and/or too stressed out from the pressures of becoming new parents to make love, then remember to be flexible with yourselves on what you can give each other. Just holding hands, or hugging each other and kissing, or giving each other back rubs or foot massages can help to ease the tension and keep you feeling close.

Practical Tips for New Parents

When kids come along, some adjustments to your life, including when and how you make love, come along, too.

Knocking and Noise

Consider teaching your children when they are young about the importance of respecting the privacy of others and always knocking—and waiting for a reply—before entering a room. Once they are old enough to grasp the concept of privacy, you may want to get a "Do Not Disturb" sign for your bedroom door to avoid spontaneous walk-ins when you are making love.

Also, many parents like to wait until they know for sure that their children have fallen fast asleep before making love. This gives them a greater chance of not being walked in on at an embarrassing moment.

If the two of you like to vocalize your pleasure during lovemaking, you might choose to moderate your enthusiasm by whispering, or by adding background music, such as slow, sexy jazz. Or you may prefer to use white noise (in the form of a fan or a humidifier) to muffle the sounds of your sexual pleasure.

Tag-Team Parenting

Couples find an effective way to give each other a break from the physical and emotional demands of childcare is to trade off with each other the parenting responsibilities. For instance, if one parent has had a particularly demanding work week, the other parent may offer to play with the kids on Saturday morning so that the exhausted parent has a chance to sleep in and relax. Or one parent may offer to take the kids to the park or zoo for a few hours on a Sunday afternoon, while the other parent uses that time to runs errands and get some housework done.

Helping each other out with parenting duties is a great way to enhance sexual desire, because it's a way to show each other how much you care. And of course you recall what we have been saying about "actions speaking louder than words." People who feel their partners are nurturing and supporting them by doing their fair share of the parenting are bound to have a greater desire for making love.

Babysitting Options

Tag-team parenting can be useful at times, but you will need the private couple time to keep your emotional and physical intimacy—the two key ingredients of your sex life—firing on all cylinders. If it becomes harder and harder to find time together, consider hiring a babysitter.

Finding a babysitter you like and trust can be challenging if you don't have family or friends nearby who can help, and it can be cost-prohibitive. One way around this predicament is to inquire at one of your local preschools or elementary schools about babysitting co-ops in your community that you could utilize. These co-ops consist of a large group of moms (and some dads) in your area who exchange babysitting services (at either no or minimal cost) with one another. If no such co-op currently exists in your area, it's an opportunity to talk with your friends and neighbors about starting one in your community.

The important thing to remember is that you need to make the effort to have couple time with your partner, and that means getting a babysitter once in a while.

Remember Your Social Life

Try not to let your social life with your friends go out the window when you become new parents. If you are reluctant to hire a babysitter, or if you have not found one who you like, you can always consider socializing with other parents whose kids are close in age to yours. In this way, you get to have some important grown-up time with your friends, while knowing that your kids are safe, well supervised, and having fun with trusted friends.

It is restorative and energizing to have a social outlet with your peers and other adults. And any restorative activity that the two of you engage in together can revitalize your sexual desire and enhance your mutual pleasure.

The Remedy for Child-Centered Households

These days, some couples place their children at the center of their universe. And while this is honorable, and certainly of great benefit to the kids, it can be hard on the couple's relationship.

Think about what happens if two partners neglect their sexual desires, emotional needs, interests, and passions, both as individuals and as a couple, and pour every last drop of their energy into their children's development. This is not a terribly balanced equation, to say the least. And couples who make this choice often end up paying a steep emotional price in their relationship at some point down the road for totally sacrificing their own needs, hopes, and dreams.

Remember that it's healthy for children to observe parents who love *each other*. When they see their parents kissing, hugging, and showing affection in their words and actions, what they are actually witnessing is healthy, loving commitment in action.

And when children see parents who are pursuing their own life dreams and career aspirations, this gives them perspective that their parents' universe doesn't revolve solely around their needs, and sets an example for the fulfillment in pursuing their own dreams when they get older.

Also, when parents are visibly happy in their relationship with each other, their children are free of worry and guilt surrounding that relationship. The kids won't feel a responsibility for trying to be everything for their parents or trying to make them happy.

You are not taking anything away from your children by giving attention to your partner. On the contrary, you are setting a wonderful example of what affection between loving partners looks like. You are saying affection is natural and comforting. Some kids grow up never seeing their parents kiss or hug. If you want your children to be comfortable with affection, they have to see it in your household.

Have you ever noticed how kids sometimes rush to push mom and dad aside when they are kissing? They just want to be included in the circle of love. Or sometimes kids close their eyes and teasingly say, "Yuck!" when they see mom and dad kissing. Teasing their parents like this is just another way for them to feel included and to express the pleasure they take in knowing how much their parents love each other.

Achieving the Ultimate Blend

Family time and couple time can co-mingle, complement, and enhance one another, rather than compete with one another. For instance, if the two of you have a regular babysitter and a standing date on Saturday nights, you have guaranteed yourselves some couple time each week. Just knowing that the two of you can count on having one uninterrupted block of time together week in and week out can work wonders for your sexual desire.

And in the same way that you may have chosen to designate Saturday nights as your date night, you may also want to designate Saturday afternoons as your family time, where you, your partner, and your kids all get together to toss a ball in the yard, or play board games, or do puzzles, or go out to lunch or a movie as a family.

Consider weekend napping as one great way to connect with your partner. Nap time can be a lovely form of couple time. And just think: during your naps the two of you can alternate between dozing and fantasizing about your next romantic getaway!

It's also a good idea to keep reminding yourself and your partner that raising children is a phase in your relationship. It's not a permanent condition, and that it doesn't have to take away from your sexual relationship.

As a couple, sharing in the joy of raising your children together is the emotional bond that keeps you going far beyond the hot passion in the bedroom. Fulfillment comes when you remember to focus on what is really important to you as a family and as a couple.

In the parenting years, life often seems overwhelming. But when you focus on what matters most—the smiles on your children's faces, the loving embrace of your partner, the house filled with laughter and excitement—you can let go of your to-do list and take in the joys of being a family.

The Least You Need to Know

◆ When children come along, couple time has to be woven in around family time.

◆ Be equally as loving and affectionate with your partner as you are with your children.

◆ Focusing on the importance of your relationship as a couple can help you cope with the major life transition of becoming parents.

◆ Maintaining strong communication and a positive outlook, keeping your sense of humor, being flexible, hiring babysitters, and maintaining your social life with your friends keeps your emotional bond and sexual desire alive.

◆ The empty-nest years often herald a resurgence of sexual desire and the discovery and rediscovery of sexual pleasures as well as life enhancing activities.

9

Work Time

In This Chapter

- ◆ Adult human beings' powerful need for satisfying love relationships and stimulating work

- ◆ How partners need to support and nurture each other's career aspirations

- ◆ The importance for partners to encourage each other to do their best work

- ◆ Managing the blurred lines between work life and home life

- ◆ Work-related problems that interfere with a couple's love relationship

In many households, both partners have careers, either inside or outside of the home. The demands and obligations of these work lives often put pressure on—and take time away from—a couple's relationship with each other.

Because work is a reality of life, something most all of us must do to live the lives we desire, it's important to explore how your work life and relationship life can be mutually enriching and actually fuel your sex life instead of extinguish it.

The Human Need for Love and Work

It was Sigmund Freud, the father of psychoanalysis, who said: "Love and work … work and love, that's all there is." He also said: "Love and work are the cornerstones of our humanness." And, last but not least, he contended that the two primary indicators of sound mental health in an adult human being are the ability to love and the ability to work.

Just as children gain a sense of competency through mastering various kinds of play, as adults, we gain our sense of competency through our accomplishments in the workplace and in our homes. We all seek fulfillment in having *both* loving relationships with our partners and interesting careers that make us feel like productive, contributing members of society.

Supporting Each Other's Careers and Dreams

You recall our discussions about the importance of individuation in love relationships. Well, one of the best ways for partners to help each other achieve healthy individuation within the relationship is to support each other's professional aspirations and dreams. In other words, when you tell your partner his career aspirations and interests are exciting and worth pursuing, and when he does this for you, your feelings of emotional intimacy with each other will deepen. And as we've discussed, anything couples can do to deepen their feelings of emotional intimacy can only serve to enhance their feelings of sexual desire.

Some people know from the age of 12 that they want to be a teacher or artist or doctor or engineer or computer whiz. They take all the necessary classes, get all the necessary degrees, and never deviate from the career path they chose all the way back in middle school. Others, however, take a more scenic route to finding their ultimate career destinations.

Let's take the case of Alex, who, at age 12, wants to be a police officer. But at age 17, he fine-tunes the idea of law enforcement and decides to pursue becoming a lawyer instead. Then, in college, he takes a class in graphic design that he enjoys so much that he decides to change gears and go to graduate school to study architecture.

Alex goes on to become a happy and professionally fulfilled architect, with no regrets about the career path he has chosen, or how he got there. But he also harbors another dream, an *avocational* one, as opposed to a vocational one: the desire to become a comedian.

Ever since he was a kid, he has enjoyed making people laugh. He has always wondered what it would be like to stand on the stage of a comedy club with a mic in his hand, under the spotlight, telling jokes that people find

def•i•ni•tion

An **avocation** is a cherished occupation or hobby that a person has in addition to his or her primary profession.

funny. It's not his ambition to go on the late-night talk show circuit, or to make his living from stand-up comedy. After all, he happens to enjoy his day job as an architect very much and the things it provides him. He'd just like to do a few gigs around town and see what happens from there.

Well, Alex has not only been fortunate enough to fulfill his professional dreams, he has been lucky in love as well. Indeed, his wife Susan has always been his number-one fan. She loves his sense of humor. In fact, she thinks it is one of his sexiest qualities, and tells him so quite often.

They met in college, and she had been the primary breadwinner for several years working as an executive recruiter while he was in graduate school. Now she is a stay-at-home mom taking care of their 2-year-old son, Billy, and Alex supports the family with his salary as an architect.

But Susan has always known about Alex's other dream of becoming a stand-up comic. He tries out his jokes on her first, and she helps him edit and tweak them until they both think the timing and rhythm of each joke is just right. Eventually, Alex feels ready to go to an open-mic night at a local club to test out some of his best material.

And little by little, Alex starts to realize his comedy dream by landing some gigs, and he firmly believes that the credit for making this dream-come-true belongs to Susan. She supported him fully by helping him revise his jokes when they weren't clicking and boosting his confidence by making him feel like a funny guy who just needed the chance to prove himself. In short, Susan always believed in Alex and his abilities. And it is her belief in him that consistently carried him through his periods of self-doubt, and helped him to believe in himself.

This example demonstrates how by supporting each other's dreams and work goals, committed couples show their love for each other, and this keeps their bonds of sexual and emotional intimacy strong. They function as each other's greatest cheerleaders, most reliable sounding boards, and, when necessary, most constructive critics.

For example, Susan would never want Alex to go on stage for the first time and bomb. So when he writes a joke that she thinks needs more work, she tells him so with loving, supportive, gentle words—not harsh, degrading, harmful ones. So he does not feel the least bit hurt by her constructive criticism. He has total faith in her taste and judgment, and knows her suggestions are not meant to derail or undermine his abilities. And second, he knows that she has only his best interests at heart.

As for her career, Susan enjoyed working in the recruitment field for a few years, but now she feels happy about staying home and taking care of their young son. She may go back to recruiting when Billy gets older. But she also has a few other career dreams as well, such as getting a Ph.D. in psychology. Whatever she ultimately decides to do, she knows that Alex will support her completely.

It's not surprising that Alex and Susan feel profoundly bonded on an emotional level. And once again, as we have been saying throughout this book, the more emotionally connected two partners feel, the more likely they will continue desiring each other sexually. In fact, this undercurrent of unconditional love and encouragement sets a positive, upbeat tone for just about everything they do together, whether it's making love, co-writing jokes, going grocery shopping, or playing hide-and-seek with their son.

Inspiring Each Other's Best Work

Many people consider their partners to be their chief source of inspiration in their lives and careers. In an article called "It Takes Two," in the February 23, 2007, issue of Entertainment Weekly, a group of reporters asked several Oscar nominees to name the one person who inspired them the most.

Some of the nominees named a director or other work colleague who had helped them move to the next level, creatively speaking. But not surprising, some of them named their spouses as their primary artistic muses and sources of inspiration.

For example, Cate Blanchett, who was nominated in the Supporting Actress category for her role in *Notes On a Scandal*, named her husband of 10 years, the playwright Andrew Upton, as her primary source of inspiration: "Andrew is the first person with whom I've been able to deeply discuss my roles. Actors can be superstitious about discussing that mysterious process of connecting text to a character, and Andrew, as a writer, can be quite illuminating and point out things I can't see. We're [involved] in each other's work and have both become better as a result. And in the end, that's all you want in any creative partnership." Cate Blanchett has deep insight into how she and her husband continually challenge and inspire each other to climb to greater and greater creative heights.

In the same article, Forest Whitaker—who later went on to win an Oscar—talks about his wife of almost 11 years, Keisha Whitaker: "I share all the details with her, including my insecurities." By disclosing that he has no trouble sharing everything—even his insecurities—with his wife, Forest Whitaker is giving us a peek into their powerful bond of emotional intimacy. And Ms. Whitaker describes her faith in her husband's ability as an actor like this: "I've seen Forest pull so many characters out of himself. I knew how intense the transformation would become."

Clearly, loving partners give each other the wings they need to fly at work, at home, and anywhere else they may travel, separately or together. The passionate spirit of creative collaboration that lies at the heart of these two examples reveals how much a couple's love for each other can enrich their work, and how much their work can enliven their love.

Think about ways you can encourage and support your partner in his line of work and life interests. Also think about how he supports you in yours. Also, when you both recognize and show appreciation for the unique talents and gifts in each other, this is offering your love and support to each other, and will enable you both to flourish in what you love to do and strengthen your bond as a couple.

Career Change Is Inevitable

The era of working for one employer until retirement is long gone. According to research on work trends conducted by the U.S. Department of Labor and other organizations, nowadays most people can expect to make multiple career changes before they retire. The latest data from the National Longitudinal Study of Youth that began in 1979, (an ongoing longitudinal study of men and women born between 1957 and 1964), indicates the average number is about ten different jobs for workers between the ages of 18 and 38. Of course, statistics like this mean that nowadays many people can expect to make multiple career changes before they retire.

In addition, various economic factors can lead to job loss and/or career reevaluation, either or both of which can instigate a career change. And of course, as we've been saying, it's important for partners to support each other through any of these changes.

This is one reason it is so important for partners to be patient and encouraging with each other during the various career transitions that, statistically speaking, most of them are likely to experience.

Love Booster

When you and your partner support each other's career aspirations, you give each other the strength and stamina you both need to succeed professionally. You also function as a loving, supportive "team of two," which can only further enhance your mutual feelings of sexual desire.

Blurred Lines Between Work and Home

In these times, many people find that the line between work life and home life has grown blurry. For example, let's take the case of Pam. A wife and mother, Pam has opened up a flower shop in town. She has invested a big chunk of her family's nest egg in the costs of opening the store, and she needs to start turning a profit as quickly as possible.

There is also a larger chain flower shop in town, so she is competing with it for business. She has hired an excellent assistant, Ann. But Pam is the one who still ends up doing most of the little extra things essential to getting a new business off the ground.

In terms of Pam's day-to-day reality, this means that she takes work-related calls from customers and vendors at all hours, day or night, whether she is at home or at the store. She even takes calls on her cell phone when she and her husband Jack are out on their weekly date night, having dinner at their favorite local restaurant, or when she is helping her daughter Ashley with homework.

In other words, the phone calls never, ever stop. Jack and Ashley try their hardest to be understanding, but Pam knows that the current situation is tough on everyone. And she often finds herself wondering: "How much longer can my family be expected to put up with this?"

For instance, how does Jack feel when Pam takes work-related calls while they are out on their date nights? He tolerates it, of course, because he loves and supports her, and he wants her business to succeed. But at the same time, it has become a source of some tension between them.

Similarly, how does Ashley feel when Pam takes a call from a customer right in the middle of a homework session? Ashley probably feels she's not very high on her mom's priority list. Of course, Pam has no intention of making Ashley feel this way. But she has made a series of work-related choices that have led to this situation.

And now she knows that she has to make some adjustments to make things better. Such as, even though it would be costly, she could hire a second assistant so that she no longer has to field all of the after-hours calls, or set up a schedule with Ann to take the calls at certain times, and she'll take them at others—this would help give some predictability to her evenings and ability to plan accordingly. Most important, Pam is recognizing that she is not fully present with the ones she loves when she wants to be and is expected to be, and she wants to do something about it.

It's not humanly possible to establish and maintain an absolutely perfect balance between your work life and your home life. Inevitably, there will be days when you feel you are juggling too many balls in the air at once. But there are ways to set better boundaries between your work life and home life.

For example, designate certain times as uninterrupted couple time, and other times as uninterrupted family time, and no matter what, these times are devoted exclusively to that time. Your partner and children will thank you for it, and ultimately, so you will you.

Remember, a big part of enhancing sexual desire comes down to you and your partner feeling that your relationship with each other is top priority. So try not to accept work-related calls during or after a certain time. And try not to read and reply to too many work-related e-mails when you're at home having family time, and consider not bringing your laptop with you the next time you go on a family vacation or a romantic getaway. All of the above can lead to a big pay-off with your partner in the bedroom!

When Both Partners Work at Home

In this Internet era, many people work out of home-based offices, and in some households, both partners work at home. Maybe one runs a business from home and the other is a freelance writer, or one designs websites and the other is an events planner. In such households, the line between a couple's personal life and work life can become very blurry when both work at home, so it's a good idea to set boundaries and ground rules right from the beginning.

For instance, if you have enough space, set up two separate offices. This way, you won't be tripping over each other or disturbing each other when one of you is on the phone and the other is concentrating on writing a report.

When you both work at home, a benefit is you can take breaks together. Occasionally let these coffee breaks turn into kissing breaks, and lunch breaks turn into lovemaking breaks. And why not? It's a great opportunity if the kids are at school, and your energy level may be higher in the middle of the day than at the end of a busy day. Even on days when you are both too busy to take love breaks—you feel lucky if you can grab a sandwich at your respective desks—you can still sneak into each other's offices for a quick kiss, chat, or back rub.

When Partners Are Colleagues

We recently had the good fortune of interviewing a woman named Kathleen via e-mail. She is the managing director and co-founder of a creative agency/production company and her husband, Christian, is the creative director and co-founder. We wanted to know how spouses who work together manage to distribute their time among the three main categories of couple time, family time, and work time, as this is the case when all of these aspects could easily get blurred into one.

Kathleen's insights about how it's good for couples to approach every area of their lives in a spirit of collaboration and teamwork sheds light on how *all* couples—not just couples who work together—can achieve a greater sense of harmony and balance between their work lives and their home lives.

In Kathleen's words, "Christian and I don't just work together; we are entrepreneurs together. And the success and stability of our family financial situation rests on the success of our business. We can't blame the boss or the company for foolish decisions or crazy deadlines because we are the boss. If things slide or fail, we are the people who suffer first and foremost.

"The benefit, however, of this situation is that neither one of us nags the other about our work commitments—we automatically understand why work is being done and understand and agree about the trade-offs that sometimes have to be made. So in that respect I think it's a much more supportive situation than we had when we both worked separately at other businesses."

Kathleen believes, "that marriage is about so much more than just being in love. Christian and I could love a great many people, but I think that we could only be married to each other. In my opinion, the enterprise that is marriage is built on a lot of seemingly basic and boring, but critical, beliefs surrounding priorities, lifestyle, and value systems. We're in sync on how these beliefs shake out, so we're able to make decisions about what we do and how we prioritize things. Couple time, family time, and work time are often co-mingled. In fact, one of the driving forces behind building our own company was the financial need for me to work and the desire to create a work environment where I could earn a living, but still be physically home for our children."

Kathleen also observes, "As our kids get older, their needs shift—and our thoughts about my need to be physically located with them shift, too. And these changes open up more opportunities to carve out couple time. For instance, starting this year I work 1 day a week in the city (instead of at home). So now, when we commute together on the train, the time we spend on the commute might be devoted to dealing with work issues one week or talking about current events the next. When I'm in the city, we might eat with the staff one week, and the next week go out to lunch separately to have a conversation about the children or maybe a book we've read. Our lives are very integrated without being suffocating. I truly know what challenges he's facing and he knows mine."

How do they manage to find time in their busy schedules for dates? She says, "We hire a 'mother's helper' to look after the kids for about 2 hours every other Sunday and we go out for coffee. The only rule we have is that we can't talk about the company then. We also try to do a date once a month. We set once a month as our goal and then we probably end up actually managing it once every other month. The important thing here is that we use this once-a-month date goal as a tool, but not as a measure of success or failure. There are altogether too many opportunities in this life to measure oneself and come up short, so I think it's important to make sure that things we envision as motivators don't morph into measurements or, worse, weapons."

When discussing the joys of working with her husband, Kathleen says, "I feel very close to Christian and I know what he's actually doing every day. What clients, vendors, or staff people are proving to be challenging. He knows the same about me, so it gives us the opportunity to be sensitive and supportive and kind in a way that we might not be able to be if our lives weren't so intermingled."

And with regard to the challenges that can come along with working together, she observes, "Sometimes I have to have difficult conversations with him in my role as the business strategist and operations manager. I have had to tell him that he's got to change his behavior. Those aren't easy conversations to have, but I think it is a real credit to Christian that he knows I'm giving him hard feedback because it's ultimately in his best interest. He does the same for me, but given our roles—he's the Creative Director—I'm often the one giving the hard messages. I've also had to make financial decisions that have an impact on the creative [product] that he produces, and those discussions are quite energetic and lively—but strictly professional. We both know that you can't bring home issues into the work place—or vice versa."

Overall, she loves the fact that, "We both share in our successes and triumphs. When we win an award, *we* really win. When we get press or an article gets picked up, we're really proud of each other. I'm Christian's biggest fan and I think he's mine. I really admire him and respect him and I truly feel that he respects and admires me. We do have separate roles and so we keep to our own bailiwicks, so I think that probably helps a lot."

They also refuse to play the blame game, and they place a lot of emphasis on working together as an indivisible team. Or, as Kathleen says, "It also helps that when we fail, we fail together, and we work to rescue situations as a team. No blaming is allowed. I've always felt that you learn more about teamwork from being on a losing team than on a winning one—and I've certainly found that it's precisely when we've had our greatest challenges that I've found what a wonderful partner I have in Christian."

Kathleen and Christian are a great example of how couples can successfully work together but not at the expense of their relationship and family. If you noticed, Kathleen talked a lot about how they communicate, both when and about what. If you and your partner work together or plan to work together at some point, keep communicating!

How Work Interferes with Love

So far we've discussed the positive ways in which a couple's love for each other can enhance their work lives and vice versa. It's also important to touch on some of the work-related problems that can harm a couple's love relationship.

Work Burnout

We all fundamentally know we need to strive to strike a healthy balance in our love life, work life, and family life. At the same time, numerous work-related issues have the potential to sabotage our emotional and physical health, as well as our relationship with our partners.

Identifying some work-related problems can help hone in on what is driving a strain on your love relationship:

- Having a job that you despise

- Not making enough money; worrying about finances all of the time

- Feeling that you are in a dead-end job with no chance for career growth or promotion

- Having a difficult boss and/or colleagues who make your work life unpleasant on a consistent basis

- Being harassed or bothered in any way (including sexually) at work

- Worrying about job security

- Working in an environment that is physically dangerous

- Having a job in which your income is based on commissions rather than on a steady, reliable salary

- Working at a job that is tedious, repetitive, and/or boring

- Having a job with a poorly defined or endlessly changing job description

- Working in a job where you don't feel adequately supported, nurtured, or appreciated

If you are currently experiencing any of these problems, you may be or are becoming depressed, agitated, and difficult to be around. When a problem at work becomes so overwhelming that it takes over your entire life, it may be time to take a step back, re-evaluate your career goals, and start brainstorming with your partner, family members, and friends about possible short-term and long-term solutions.

People who become depressed about their job situation can also develop a sense of hopelessness and inadequacy that carry over to the bedroom. For the sake of your health and your relationship with your partner, it is important to assess how you feel at work and about your work, seek help if necessary, and make adjustments.

When Work Is Your Whole Identity

Many of us identify strongly with what we do for a living. It's even reflected in the language we use to describe our occupations. For instance, we tend to say, "I am a teacher," rather than "My job is teaching" or "I work as a teacher."

Some mental health professionals and spiritual advisors maintain that too many of us identify too strongly with our careers. They wonder, "Why can't we just 'be'?" After all, we are human beings, not human doings. Why must our jobs be such a big part of how we define ourselves as individuals?

Well, it's easy to see why work can become such a significant part of a person's identity. Many people devote years of training and education to entering certain professions. These positions may require them to put in many hours at the office. When they start moving along on their career paths, they may push themselves harder and harder to achieve more and more, to get that promotion or that raise, or to get more praise and attention from their bosses.

To put it bluntly, we live in a society of overachievers, and there is both internal and external pressure to keep up. It's no wonder, then, that our work becomes such an integral component of our identities.

Mood Killer

Excessive multi-tasking is stressful and not something to take into the bedroom. It can only lead to inattentiveness and distractedness during lovemaking, which does not serve either partner well. Enjoyable lovemaking with your partner requires your full attention and total emotional presence.

People who identify too strongly with their careers, however, often end up paying a very steep emotional price for making this choice. Their partners, children, and friends don't see enough of them, let alone feel connected to them, and they get too stressed out too often. Also they may lose their perspective about what matters most in life: their relationships with their partners and other loved ones.

So while it's normal in our society to feel like your work is your iden-tify, it's important to remember who you are and what's important to you in this world. This will enable you to maintain a healthy balance in your life and love relationship.

Being a Workaholic

All of this brings us to a related problem of workaholism. A "worka-holic" is someone who lives to work, rather than works to live. People who spend an excessive amount of time and energy on their careers at the expense of their relationships are considered workaholics. Essentially, they are addicted to their work.

> **Notable Quotable**
>
> "Ask yourself this key question: *Just what is it you're working for?* When all is said and done, no one has ever devoted their last gasping words to the wish, 'If only I'd spent more of my life working.'"
> —Eve Salinger, author of *The Complete Idiot's Guide To Pleasing Your Man*

While it is highly desirable to have a career that you enjoy, if your work has become the primary source of joy and satisfaction in your life or your partner's life, you or your partner may be shutting yourselves off from experiencing more personal and intimate forms of happiness, such as a rich, satisfying sex life with each other.

Think about it. If you devote too much time and energy to your job, your partner will start to feel lonely and neglected. After all, as we've discussed, all people want to feel they are at the top of their partner's priority list.

So if you and/or your partner feel you are virtually married to your work, then you may need to take stock of your life goals. Talk to each other, to good friends, or to a therapist about your desire to restore a healthy balance between your work life and your intimate life with your partner.

Mood Killer

People who work all the time often expend most of their passion and energy before they reach the bedroom. If you spend a lot of time working, remember it's also important to devote plenty of your time and energy to lovemaking, conversation and companionship with your partner.

The Least You Need to Know

◆ People need both love relationships and satisfying careers to feel truly fulfilled as adult human beings.

◆ Partners who support, nurture, and encourage each other's careers are most likely to experience a strong sexual desire and an enjoyable sex life.

◆ The blurry lines between work life and home life can be positive or negative for enhancing your sexual desire and healthy growth of your love relationship, depending on how you handle them.

◆ Work-related problems including stress, lack of fulfillment, and burnout can have a negative impact on sexual desire and other aspects of a couple's love relationship.

Chapter 10

Sexual Teamwork

In This Chapter

- ◆ The Three Ts of sexual teamwork
- ◆ How to be a sexual team player
- ◆ Using sex codes and signals with your partner
- ◆ Finding the type and quantity of sex that works for you
- ◆ The key tips and strategies for enhancing your sexual desire

In this final chapter, we'll share with you what you need to know about "sexual teamwork" and the pleasures of bringing a sexually collaborative spirit to the bedroom. With your new spirit and attitude, you'll be able to approach each new sexual experience with your partner with what the Zen Buddhists call a "Beginner's Mind."

We'll also examine the "Three Ts of sexual teamwork," and pull together all the love-boosting ideas, tips, and strategies we've discussed together so you can rev up your sexual desire and take your sex life with your partner to a thrilling new level of erotic excitement and mutual satisfaction. Indeed, when you work together as a fully united sexual team, the two of you will discover all sorts of sexy, wonderful ways to make your love life continuously exciting and intimate.

Creating a Sexual Partnership

A sexual partnership begins when both partners recognize the need to work together to create a mutually satisfying sexual relationship. Couples who agree to form this sexual partnership are on the right path to creating a juicy, satisfying sex life. When the two of you are willing to overcome your sexual inhibitions and are willing to reveal your innermost physical and emotional turn-ons, you are creating a partnership that will keep your sex life vibrant. This blending of your deepest erotic desires with your partner's enables you both to find the best ways to express and enjoy your sexuality together.

If you are both willing to learn how to communicate about your sexual feelings, then the two of you are taking the first wonderful steps toward creating a lasting bridge to sexual passion. If you are open and vulnerable when it comes to expressing your deepest sexual wishes, you can achieve your shared goal of mutually satisfying sex. And what could be more fun and exciting than that?

Love Booster

As the two of you work together on sexual teamwork, keep this acronym in mind: PAIRS = a Playful Attitude Is Relaxing and Sexy.

Just as you both need to talk openly about what gives you sexual pleasure, you also need to be able to talk openly about those aspects of sex that make you feel anxious, fearful, inhibited, embarrassed, or ashamed. Talking directly and honestly with your partner can help you both clarify any specific issues or inhibitions that may be preventing either of you from enjoying yourselves to the fullest-possible extent during lovemaking.

The Three Ts of Sexual Teamwork

Sexual teamwork is made up of the Three Ts—time-talk-touch. This is making time for your lovemaking, talking with your partner about it, and touching each other in sexually stimulating ways that help to enhance your mutual desire. These Three Ts pull together the concepts we've explored in great detail throughout this book.

Time

Of the three areas we've discussed that contributes uniquely to your overall sense of fulfillment as a human being—couple time, family time, and work time—couple time is essential for a healthy relationship, but unfortunately, it is the area that ends up being neglected most often.

You won't neglect your work because that would be irresponsible. And of course you won't neglect your children because that would be criminal. So in the same way it's unacceptable to neglect your work and your family, it's unacceptable to neglect your love life with your partner. Everything you care about—and that certainly includes your sex life with your partner—requires your loving, nurturing attention.

Whenever you feel your relationship with your partner getting short-changed, review and implement the practical tips and strategies for couple time in Chapter 7.

Also, take another look at family time in Chapter 8 and work time in Chapter 9 to remember the specific ways you can harmonize and balance your couple time with your family and work time.

Even the simple act of letting your partner know that you are eager to make more time for your love life will tell him that you are prioritizing him and your relationship. Knowing how much you care is sure to make him feel adored and appreciated. Not only that, but when you make a point of prioritizing your love relationship, you are bound to feel more enthusiastic about it yourself. And when you approach your sex life with an enthusiastic, appreciative mindset, you will boost your sexual desire and pleasure.

Talk

Communicating continuously creates a sexual road map for you and your partner. Sharing exactly what you both enjoy doing in bed is the beginning of your journey. And while talking about sex is not always easy, it can be very exciting.

"Let's try this," you can say. "Oh, I like it when you touch me there," she can respond. "Ahhh, that feels great," you can whisper. "How can I touch you in a satisfying way? Does this feel good?" he can ask.

Such simple signals convey messages of pleasure. And these messages are vital feedback for creating mutually satisfying sexual experiences together.

Of course the two of you don't have to stick to any one rigid, carefully plotted-out path to mutual sexual satisfaction every time you make love. A sexual road map can change, adapt, and deviate whenever you like, to suit your needs and desires.

Whatever new techniques or scenarios you decide to try, be sensitive to your partner's willingness or lack of willingness, as well as your lover's comfort zone. There's an expression that says, "It takes two to tango." You can't tango if one of you really isn't in the mood. Sexual trust is built on mutual respect for each other's erotic desires and boundaries.

Remember, it always comes back to sexual teamwork. The two of you share a common goal: your mutual sexual pleasure. This is why it's a good idea for both of you to speak as openly and honestly as possible about what you enjoy the most, and which activities or scenarios you might be open to trying. Make this your couple motto: "If you don't ask for what you want, you might not get what you need." Or, "We ask for what we want so that we get what we need."

If there is an erotic scenario you play out in your mind that you would love to act out, say so! Similarly, if there is something your partner would like to try, keep an open mind and heart when she communicates it. Be ready to be persuaded!

Touch

Speaking of sexual road maps, think of your own body and your lover's body as a pair of beautiful landscapes. Think of your partner as a bold sexual explorer who wants to discover and sexually please every inch of you.

The most important element in sex is hands. Not many people know that. Having sensitive hands will do more to make your lover appreciate you than anything else—unless of course you are a virtuoso with all of your equipment.

Everyone is hungry for sensitive, caring, delicate touching. If you want to be a good lover, you really ought to investigate touching as much as possible. There are many different ways of touching, and you might be surprised by how much there is to learn. Here is a touching exercise to try with your partner to explore the sexual power of simple, slow touching. Take off your clothes and lie facing each other on the bed or wherever you are comfortable. Gaze deeply into each other's eyes as you both slowly and teasingly run your fingers up and down every inch of each other's bodies. Start with massaging each other's scalps. Run your fingers through each other's hair. Tune in to the feel of your fingers on each other's scalps.

If you feel like closing your eyes, or tipping your head back, or moaning, give in to your urges. These urges are your body's natural way of expressing its appreciation for your lover's touch on your skin, as well as the feel of his skin beneath yours. After running your fingers gently through each other's hair, let your fingers slide down each other's temples and cheeks. Give each other's noses a playful squeeze. Trace the arched shapes of each other's eyebrows.

You may notice yourselves spontaneously smiling, or even laughing. You may also notice your bodies relaxing into the exercise. Move your fingers slowly down each other's necks. Give in to the tingle.

Remember the places where both of your fingers have just been, as they may be erogenous zones for either or both of you. An exercise like this can help you discover just where and how you most like to be touched. It can wake up your senses, get your skin tingling, and set your passion aflame.

After you have run your fingers along the backs, sides, and fronts of each other's necks, slip your hands down to each other's shoulders. This is a place where you may both be holding some pent-up tension, so don't hesitate to rub and massage each other's shoulders. And again, if you feel like letting out a moan of pleasure, give in to your urge, as it can only enrich the experience further for both of you.

Next, move your hands to each other's chests, caressing each other softly and tenderly. Then slip your hands down to the small of each other's backs, another profoundly erogenous zone for many people. Slide your hands along each other's hips. Tune in to the contours of your body and his. Next, move your hands down to each other's thighs, knees, and calves.

For a teasingly tantalizing sensation, stroke very lightly, up and down, with just the tips of your fingers. And finally, stroke each other's feet and toes. If either or both of you are ticklish, give in to your laughter. After all, tickling each other and making each other laugh are two more wonderful ways to wake up each other's senses and feel fully alive.

After you perform this kind of desire-enhancing exercise in mindful sensuality, both of you will probably be feeling extremely turned on, and very much in the mood for more intimate touching, so don't be shy. In other words, now that you are both worked up, this would be the time to start engaging in more direct sexual touching and actual lovemaking. After all, enhancing your mutual sexual desire is what this exercise is all about, so go for it!

Being a Sexual Team Player

Differing levels of sexual desire is one of the most common problems for which couples seek professional help from marriage counselors or sex therapists. When one partner wants sex and the other one refuses, relationship problems can develop. So this is when being a sexual team player is critical in a relationship.

The best sex comes not from forcing it but from allowing it—allowing the sexual energy between the two of you to move you. Good sex is like dancing: listening to the music and letting your body move with its rhythm. It's like hearing the beat of each other's music and then dancing in tune with it—with one another. Working together in this "dance" instead of against it, by being in tune with and giving your partner what he needs and desires at any given sexual encounter, is being a sexual team player. Don't think of your partner as doing something *to* you. Think of your lover as doing something *with* you—that you are always a team in your sexual experiences together.

We describe the various physical, psychological, and emotional causes of—and medical and nonmedical treatments for—low and no sexual desire in Appendix B. Being a sexual team player is also seeking understanding about what you and/or your partner may be experiencing in terms of these types of changes in sexual desire.

Fortunately, however, as we have been discussing throughout the book, there are a variety of easy and natural ways to boost sexual desire. Because everyone is different, you may need to explore several different options before finding your own particular path to Sexytown.

It's Funny What Turns You Both On

In Chapter 4, we talked about physical turn-ons. Maybe you have discovered that reading an erotic book or watching a scene from a sexy mainstream movie can be counted on to start your sexual motor running. Or perhaps wearing a silky negligee is the surest way to make you feel all tingly, amorous, and ready for love. Whatever turns you and your partner on, it's important to explore and learn what they are as part of your sexual partnership.

By the way, one of the biggest turn-ons for people is when their partners think they are funny and clever—this feeling can up the sexual voltage almost instantly. "What really turns me on," we've heard women say, "is when a man sees me as really very funny." And men feel exactly the same way.

When someone understands your sense of humor, there's an instant fusion, because you know that they know you, that they "get" you. They know your heart, and that you're intelligent, unique, and fun to be with. They dig you, and this makes you feel spectacular. Try saying to your lover: "You're really very funny," and watch for a blush of pleasure light up his face. It's an incredible delight, and sexually arousing, when someone recognizes and appreciates you as a funny, witty individual.

Sexual Fantasies and Scenarios

Also, sexual teamwork involves sharing and understanding each other's sexual fantasies and dreams. Kinky or not, weird or not, look at them as you do a movie, and avoid judgment and revulsion. Whatever your fantasy may be, it offers a peek into your secret desires. Think of your sexual fantasies as entertainment and as hints about what new adventures might turn you on.

Above all, try not to withhold anything that is on your mind from your lover. In other words, don't shut your lover out. Let her in on your fantasies. Acting out some of your favorite sexual fantasies together is a lot like playing make-believe.

> **Notable Quotable**
>
> "With fantasy, the two of you can transport yourselves to anywhere at any time and make love in any personae. Using your imaginations in tandem can not only be erotically stimulating but also bring a deeper level of intimacy to your relationship."
>
> —Eve Salinger, author of *The Complete Idiot's Guide To Pleasing Your Man*

For many couples, fantasizing about and/or acting out various erotic scenarios is a dependable way to increase their mutual desire for lovemaking. After all, when couples allow themselves to try on various sexy roles or identities that are vastly different from their real-life personalities (a rogue pirate or naughty nurse, for example), they might feel free to do and say things they might not usually do or say. Indeed, being willing to temporarily slip out of the ordinary and into the fantasy world of erotic scenarios is sexual teamwork that can lead to unparalleled levels of sexual desire and anticipation.

Have Enthusiasm for Sex

Being a team player also involves heading into the bedroom with a positive, upbeat, and up-for-trying-anything attitude.

In Chapter 6, we discussed positive sexual self-talk versus negative sexual self-talk. Remember, *you* are the one with the power to talk yourself either into or out of just about anything. So be sure to use positive self-talk to talk yourself into trying whatever it takes to boost your sexual desire.

Let your partner know how much you appreciate his team spirit. He will certainly appreciate your positive attitude, your effort, and your willingness to explore new sexual frontiers as a sexual team. And you will be happy, too, because you will feel empowered and excited about taking positive charge of your own sexual desire and fulfillment.

Notable Quotable _____

"Each day we make a 'conscious contact' to begin the day.
Usually holding each other for a few minutes and breathing
together .... Every month there is one BIG night where we put aside four
hours to luxuriate in sex. Bathing, massaging, pleasuring of the man for
an hour, then something for the woman .... Marc and I 'soul gaze'; we
sit and face each other making eye contact. We lay our hands right
hand up, left down, gently touching. Then we breathe together. As I
expel breath Marc takes a breath in and we get into a rhythm ....This is
an amazing healing process. It still catches me off guard and melts my
fears of intimacy."
—Sally, 51

Sex Codes and Signals

Some partners develop a special form of sex communication or code
for sex to let each other know when they are in the mood—or might be
persuaded to get in the mood—for making love.

For instance, you could say to your partner, "It's thong-time," and this
may be all you need to say to let him know you are wearing a pair of
thong panties that are making you feel sexy and eager to make love.

It is so much fun to send sexy signals and talk in sex code with your
partner before you ever enter the bedroom. You are building up anticipation, so that by the time the two of you actually go to bed, you will
feel as amorous and excited as a couple of newlyweds!

Speaking of newlyweds, in Chapter 1, we described the various phases
that couples experience. In the beginning of a relationship, there may
be barely any need for a sex code or other playful, sexy stimulants,
because during the honeymoon phase, you both tend to feel ready to
get busy just about all of the time!

But as life goes on, responsibilities and obligations mount, and schedules get crowded. This is precisely when this strategy of naughty sex
codes and signals, like thongs and silky negligees, erotic scenarios and
sexy books and movies, can help send the sex message and get your
juices flowing, and keep them flowing.

Take Control of Your Sexual Desire

The next time you find yourself thinking you are too tired or stressed out to make love, try not to cave in to these negative factors that can impede your sexual desire.

We have never heard anyone complain, "I'm so tired. I stayed up all night making love." On the contrary! If you have ever made love all night and gone to work in the morning beaming like a newlywed, you probably remember how radiant the world was that day. Connecting with your lover in those precious, mysterious late-night and early-morning hours is enough to turn worry upside down.

So let your stress and fatigue know that you are fighting back! You are sick and tired of feeling sick and tired, and you are not going to take it anymore! Refuse to be robbed of your sexual desire and sexual pleasure with your partner for one moment longer. Sex is too important to be allowed to slip out of your grasp day after day and night after night.

Another helpful "take control" strategy is to consciously stop thinking of desire in oversimplified, black-and-white terms, as in, you are simply either in the mood for love or not. If you think you are not, try thinking about it in terms of a big gray area in which you could be convinced to get in the mood.

> **Love Booster**
>
> Don't think in black and white. Don't think you are either "in the mood" or "out of the mood" for making love. Instead, think: "I could get into the mood by being seduced by my lover." Or else think: "I could get into the mood by being the one to seduce my lover."

Sure, maybe you're feeling a little tired because you've had a busy day. But this is your chance to take control and remind yourself of all the wonderful benefits of sex: it relaxes you and energizes you at the same time; it gives you a much-needed opportunity to be playful with your partner; it's good exercise; and it's a powerful way to connect deeply with your partner physically, emotionally, and spiritually. When you are melting into your partner, thoughts of your to-do list vanish, and that is such a pleasant relief!

So a form of taking charge is actually allowing yourself to be cajoled and seduced by your loving partner instead of giving in to your stress and fatigue—especially since what you likely need most is some loving sex and intimacy with your partner.

A "Beginner's Mind" Approach

Zen Buddhism includes a concept called "Shoshin," which involves approaching each experience with the freshness and eagerness of a "beginner's mind." In other words, eliminate preconceptions and replace them with the natural curiosity and openness of a neophyte. This concept applies beautifully to your sexual relationship with your partner.

Is it possible, after several years together, to feel as though the two of you are locked into a boring sexual routine that never changes? Sure, it's possible to feel this way. But you can change this if you bring an open mind, a beginner's mind, and an open heart to each and every new sexual experience with each other.

For example, in the same way no two snowflakes can ever be exactly alike, no single sexual experience can ever be totally identical to any other. This holds true even if you and your partner follow the same routine every single time you make love.

Let's say every time your partner kisses the back of your neck it sends shivers of excitement up your spine. But your beginner's mind will tell you that no single neck-kissing session can ever be exactly like any other the two of you have shared. Therefore, with each fresh neck-kissing session, you have the opportunity to let it lift you to brand new, unprecedented heights of sexual sensation and excitement.

Quality, Not Quantity

Frequent sex can be fantastic, but it is not always possible, given the hectic, tiring, stressful lives that many people lead these days. So it may help to remember that the overall quality of the sex that the two of you have may actually be more important than the frequency of your sexual encounters.

Of course, how the two of you define high-quality sex is personal and subjective. But chances are, especially if you have been together for a while, you have a keen sense of what feels good for each of you, both emotionally and physically.

Avoid Comparisons

It's not about how often you do it, but rather how lovingly and enthusiastically you do it. It's about the quality of your energy for one another, and the quality of your attention and interest. A lot of couples say, "What really turned me on was that my lover and I were in sync." And this genuinely attentive interest has a lot to do with the quality of your sexual activity.

There's no need to stress about "keeping up with the Joneses" in the bedroom. Sex quizzes you read about in *Cosmo* and other gossipy magazines and their statistics are not relevant to your relationship. You may have noticed that this book contains no tables or charts about frequency of sex.

> **Mood Killer**
>
> Worrying about what other people may or may not be doing in their bedrooms is not a great way to get yourself in the mood for love. Shut out all those negative thoughts, focus on your partner and yourself and on what works best for the two of you, both sexually and emotionally.

Also, there are no pictures or graphics because they often raise, rather than lower, people's anxiety levels about sex. And of course that's the last thing we want to do! We want to take stress *out* of your sex lives, and show you just how *stress-relieving* sex can be.

So please avoid asking yourself questions like: "How often should we be having sex?" Or "What is a 'normal' or 'standard' number of times for couples to engage in sexual activity each week or each month?" None of these statistics has any bearing on your sexual relationship. It's whatever works for just the two of you.

Don't feel bad about your sex life if it's different than what you hear or read about others' sex lives—don't compare yourselves to others. Experience teaches that sex improves the more you're able to appreciate what you've already got.

Keep Sex Front and Center

Sometimes you may not be having as much sex as you would like for reasons that may be beyond your control. It could be that you or your partner travels a lot for work, or maybe one of you is recovering from surgery, or perhaps an in-law has had to move in with you and changed how you both operate at home. For whatever reason, it is important to keep sex on the radar screen of your lives as much as possible, even if you can't have it as much as you'd like.

For instance, allow yourself to fantasize while running errands. It can certainly make grocery shopping a lot more fun! Also, make a point to hug, kiss, caress, and massage each other whenever you can, and talk intimately and sexily, or even joke around about sex, to keep your sexual connection alive and your love life front and center.

Each conversation the two of you have presents a fresh chance for intimate talk. For instance, say your lover calls you up for some comfort after a rough meeting while she is on the road. This is a golden opportunity for you to listen to what's on her mind, to tell her how proud you are of her for working so hard, that you believe in her and support her in what she has to do for work. Then tell her how much she turns you on and all of the sexy things you want to do with her when she gets home!

Take Your Time

One path to quality sex is to relax. Relaxing enables you to make friends with your sexual feelings in an entirely new way. When you relax, the energy grows and grows until you experience yourself and your partner at the center of an ocean of contentment. When your focus is on relaxing together at the end of your day, you won't need to push for sexual connection; it arises naturally and with ease.

If you tend to run around all day long, putting everyone else's needs above your own, then allow yourself to relax and slow down, and put yourself in the state of relaxed readiness as we discussed earlier in the book. It will make your lovemaking with your partner a more pleasurably prolonged and quality experience.

Once the house is quiet and you have time to spend together, you may want to turn on romantic music and try some deep breathing to shift gears and wash away the cares of the day.

Before making love, each time you inhale and exhale, imagine your partner's arms around you and the feel of his breath on your skin. Then take him in your arms and start gently kissing and cuddling. Allow the passion to grow at its own sweet, slow pace.

When it comes to couple time, this is the part of the day that is reserved just for the two of you and no one else, which means that you can stretch out your foreplay for as long as you want.

You know what "they" say (and what we say, too): "Life is more about the journey than the destination." Well, the same can be said of making love with your partner.

> ### Notable Quotable
>
> "We are strong advocates of intercourse and orgasm, but there is more to 'real sex' than that. The core of sexuality is giving and receiving pleasure-oriented touching. Desire, intimacy, pleasure and satisfaction are more important than intercourse and orgasm."
>
> —Barry and Emily McCarthy, authors of *Rekindling Desire: A Step by Step Program to Help Low-Sex and No-Sex Marriages*

Indeed, the slow, leisurely type of lovemaking is all about the journey, about that delicious sense of building and building, like a beautiful musical crescendo. This is what makes slowing down—when your schedules permit—so worthwhile, and why emphasizing the quality of your lovemaking can be so sexually exciting.

When You Don't Have Time

Of course, slow, tender lovemaking is great if you have the time, and if that's what you and your partner most enjoy. But on many occasions, time is of the essence, or you both may want lovemaking that is quicker and more fiery and intense. These types of scenarios can have just as much quality to them as the slower, more drawn-out ones.

A variety of experiences add to the quality of lovemaking that a couple can have. Five-minute quickies here and there are just as important as an entire evening of lovemaking.

At this point in your relationship, you two may already have, or are starting to develop, a pretty clear sense of what you both like best in terms of foreplay, techniques, positions, intensity level, and duration. Whatever your preferences are, remember not to let time constraints keep you from enjoying satisfying sex together. A host of interruptions and unexpected circumstances are always around the corner, so getting skilled at a quickie and knowing you can always pick up where you left off later are tremendous assets to a quality sex life.

Have Reasonable Expectations

It's not a good idea to expect every single sexual encounter with your partner to totally knock your socks off. Some experiences will be okay; some will be good; and, happily, some will be off-the-charts amazing. No matter what the experience is, remember, there is quality in this time you spend together making love, whether it's orgasmic or not, and that's what's important.

Keeping your expectations realistic will help to enhance your sexual desire, too. There is such a thing as maintenance sex, or the kind of sex that just keeps the juices flowing and keeps the two of you in practice in between the more mind-blowing encounters.

"A Quickie" Review

Let's review several key concepts we have described throughout this book to help you enhance your sexual desire.

Be a Team for Sex

When you both approach your sex life with full hearts, collaborative spirits, and the shared aspiration of making your lovemaking as fulfilling and dynamic as possible, nothing can stop the two of you from achieving your sexual goals as a couple.

In fact, when the two of you work as an indivisible team for sex, your sexual possibilities are limitless. To enhance your sexual desire and rev up your sexual team spirit, remember:

- Enthusiasm is one of the most powerful tools in your desire-building toolbox. Say "Yes! Yes! Yes!" to love, life, joy, sensuality, touching, intimacy, and sex with your partner.

- Embrace, nourish, and pamper your whole self. Caring for your skin, body, and overall health celebrates your sensual side, and spurs your sexual desire.

- Use positive, life-affirming self-talk, especially when it comes to your body image and your sex life.

- Let your imagination run wild in *all* of your erotic scenarios: the ones you keep to yourself, the ones you discuss with your partner, and the ones you choose to act out with your partner.

- Have intimate, soul-baring conversations to keep strengthening your bonds of emotional intimacy with your partner. This profound emotional connection as a couple continuously fuels and deepens your mutual feelings of sexual desire and pleasure.

- Incorporate all kinds of love gestures, both big and small, into your life with your partner, like smiling at each other; hugging and kissing; helping each other around the house; cooking a sexy, tasty meal together; giving each other back rubs; and making love in a soft, tender or a wildly passionate way.

- Seduction is a generous gesture with big pay-offs for both of you. It leaves a lasting imprint on your partner's memory and is also great for enhancing your own sexual desire and putting you in touch with your own sensuality.

- Pay attention to the three key areas of your lives—couple time, work time, and family time—and strive to maintain health boundaries and balance across them all.

- Utilize the concept of erotic flow, which involves visualizing your sexual desire and pleasure as an erotic wave that is continually flowing back and forth between you and your lover.

♦ Remember that sex is a sensory experience. Tune in to the erotic messages your five senses are sending you before and during your lovemaking with your partner.

Help for a Struggling Sexual Team

Because sexual team spirit is such an integral part of your relationship with your partner, it's important to examine what can happen when partners don't view themselves as a sexual team or don't act as one.

Some couples make the dangerous mistake of treating each other as sparring partners or adversaries, rather than as lovers and best friends. This negative approach usually leads to fighting, hostility, and resentment all around. Playing the blame game is nearly always a losing proposition, and when taken too far, it can even lead to the end of a relationship.

Here are some ways you and your partner can successfully resolve problems that might arise so that you can get back to communicating well, enjoying each other's company, and making sweet, passionate love:

♦ **Fight in private.** Fighting in front of other people hurts and embarrasses others and yourselves. Having disagreements can clear the air and help relieve tension, but fighting in public adds unnecessary complications.

♦ **Speak kindly.** Even when fighting, gentle words lead to better results. State your feelings, but don't use your words as darts. Whether you are in a public situation or a private one, sweet words sit better on ears than words that are used as weapons.

♦ **Stop arguing.** If you've been fighting a lot, focus on the positive aspects of your relationship so that good energy has the chance to bubble up, which can only lead to better communication and more fulfilling lovemaking.

♦ **Let go of grudges.** Also don't bring up old fights again and again. Grudges take too much emotional energy, which only inhibits connection and growth. When you forgive each other, your energy is freed up for lovemaking!

◆ Overlook the little things. When it comes to minor stumbling blocks and silly misunderstandings, be ready to accept each other's apologies, and your own responsibility. Say, "I forgive you." And ask, "Will you forgive me?"

◆ Work together as a team. Choosing to be in this together, means you will tackle problems—and resolve them—as a fully united, loving team.

The Least You Need to Know

◆ The Three Ts of sexual teamwork are time, talk, and touch.

◆ Sexual team players are positive and enthusiastic about their sex life, take good care of their bodies and minds, use positive self-talk, and work together to fulfill erotic fantasies.

◆ Treating each other like lovers and true partners, rather than as adversaries, is sexual teamwork.

◆ The quality of sex is more important than the quantity. Avoid comparing other people's sex lives to your own.

◆ Keep sex front and center and have reasonable expectations about sex.

Bibliography and Resources for Further Reading

Barbach, Lonnie, Ed. *The Erotic Edge: 22 Erotic Stories for Couples, Reprint Edition.* New York: Plume, 1996.

Byrd, Cherie. *Kissing School: Seven Lessons on Love, Lips, and Life Force.* Seattle, WA: Sasquatch Books, 2004.

Davis, Michele Weiner. *The Sex-Starved Marriage: Boosting Your Marriage Libido, A Couple's Guide.* New York: Simon & Shuster Paperbacks, 2003.

Didion, Joan. *The Year of Magical Thinking.* New York: Knopf, 2005.

Drury, Rebecca. *The Little Bit Naughty Book of Lap Dancing for Your Lover.* Berkeley, CA: Ulysses Press, 2006.

Ferrare, Cristina. *Okay, So I Don't Have a Headache: What I Learned (and What All Women Need to Know) about Hormones, PMS, Stress, Diet, Menopause—and Sex.* New York: St. Martin's Griffin, 1999.

Golden, Arthur. *Memoirs of a Geisha.* New York: Knopf, 1997.

Gottman, John and Nan Silver. *The Seven Principles for Making Marriage Work: A Practical Guide from the Country's Foremost Relationship Expert.* New York: Three Rivers Press, 2000.

Guiliano, Mireille. *French Women Don't Get Fat: The Secret of Eating for Pleasure.* New York: Knopf, 2004.

Holstein, Lana and David Taylor. *Your Long Erotic Weekend: Four Days of Passion for a Lifetime of Magnificent Sex, Reprint Edition.* New York: Penguin Group, 2004.

Kingma, Daphne Rose. *True Love: How to Make Your Relationship Sweeter, Deeper and More Passionate, Reprint Edition.* San Francisco, Conari Press, 2002.

Kuriansky, Judith, Ph.D. *The Complete Idiot's Guide to Tantric Sex, Second Edition.* New York: Alpha, 2004.

Laumann E, Paik A, Rosen R. "Sexual dysfunction in the United States: prevalence and predictors." *JAMA*, 1999; 281(6), pp. 537–544.

Maddi, Salvatore R. "The story of hardiness: Twenty years of theorizing, research and practice." *Consulting Psychology Journal*, 2002; Vol. 54, pp. 173–185.

McCarthy, Barry, Ph.D. and Emily McCarthy. *Rekindling Sexual Desire: A Step-by-Step Program to Help Low-Sex and No-Sex Marriages.* New York: Brunner-Routledge, 2003.

Michaels, Mark A. and Patricia Johnson. *The Essence of Tantric Sexuality.* Woodbury, Minnesota: Llewellyn Publications, 2006.

Nin, Anais. *Delta of Venus.* New York: Black Dog & Leventhal Publishers, 2006

———. *Henry and June: From "A Journal of Love"—The Unexpurgated Diary of Anaïs Nin (1931-1932), Reissue Edition.* New York: Harvest Books, 1990.

Perel, Esther. *Mating in Captivity: Reconciling the Erotic and the Domestic, First Edition.* New York: Harper Collins, 2006.

Pertot, Sandra. *Perfectly Normal: Living and Loving with Low Libido.* Emmaus, PA: Rodale Books, 2005.

Real, Terrence. *I Don't Want to Talk About It: Overcoming the Secret Legacy of Male Depression, Reprint Edition.* New York: Scribner, 1998.

———. *How Can I Get Through to You? Closing The Intimacy Gap Between Men and Women, Reprint Edition.* New York: Scribner, 2002.

Reichman, Judith, M.D. *I'm Not in The Mood: What Every Woman Should Know about Improving Her Libido.* New York: William Morrow & Co., 1998.

Richardson, Justin and Mark Schuster. *Everything You Never Wanted Your Kids to Know About Sex (But Were Afraid They'd Ask): The Secrets to Surviving Your Child's Sexual Development from Birth to the Teens, Reprint Edition.* New York: Three Rivers Press, 2004.

Ross, William Ashoka. *The Wonderful Little Sex Book.* San Francisco: Conari Press, 1992.

Salinger, Eve. *The Complete Idiot's Guide to Pleasing Your Man.* Indianapolis: Alpha, 2005.

———. *The Complete Idiot's Guide to Pleasing Your Woman.* Indianapolis: Alpha, 2006.

Schlechter, Jay, Ph.D. *Intimate Friends: An Antidote to Loneliness.* Charleston, SC: BookSurge Publishing, 2003.

Shakespeare, William. *As You Like It (Folger Shakespeare Library) Reissue Edition*. Philadelphia, PA: Washington Square Press, 2004.

———. *Twelfth Night (Folger Shakespeare Library) Reissue Edition*. Philadelphia, PA. Washington Square Press, 2004.

Tannen, Deborah. *You Just Don't Understand: Women and Men in Conversation*. New York: Harper Collins Publishers, 2001.

Trillin, Calvin. *About Alice*. New York: Random House, 2006.

Appendix B

The Case of Low or No Sexual Desire

Causes and Treatments

You may just want to give a booster shot to your already-satisfying sex life with your partner. In other words, you're just looking to add a little spice, zip, and excitement.

Or you may be struggling with a severely diminished sex drive or even no sex drive at all. In fact, studies indicate that one in three women, and possibly more—as well as some men—struggle with a low sex drive (or no sex drive) at one or more points in their lives.

Doctors and mental health professionals consider low libido and no libido not only to be a relationship problem, but a health problem as well. In this appendix, we address the various physical, psychological, and emotional factors that can cause low sex drive or no sex drive. We also discuss what you can do to successfully treat this upsetting health problem.

If you have tried several or even all of the desire-enhancing techniques described in this book and others, but you still feel that your current level of sexual desire is too low (or even nonexistent), it may be time to talk with your doctor about what might be diminishing your desire and how you can solve this problem.

Throughout this book, we discuss ways to enhance your love life and vary your sexual routine in order to increase your sexual desire. But if you or your partner are experiencing certain kinds of medical problems (such as lupus or diabetes), or emotional problems (such as depression or anxiety), then acting out erotic scenarios and exploring your physical and emotional turn-ons with your partner are probably not going to be enough to shift your sexual desire into high gear. Fortunately, you can work with your doctor to figure out ways to boost your sexual desire and treat underlying health issues.

A Sex-Drive Discrepancy

If one partner wants sex more frequently than the other, this discrepancy can put pressure on even the most loving of relationships. Not only that, but if a sex-drive discrepancy is ignored or left unaddressed, it can lead to other serious relationship problems, including infidelity and, in some cases, divorce or breaking up.

This is one reason we have talked so much about the importance of being willing to engage in sex play with your partner even when you are not in the mood. Engaging in foreplay is one of the most effective ways to jumpstart your sexual desire.

As was mentioned in the book, the order of sexual activity was once believed to be that a person had to experience desire first, then arousal, then orgasm, and finally satisfaction.

But researchers now know that arousal can, and in many cases often does, precede desire. More specifically, sexual arousal—in the form of kissing and cuddling and sexual foreplay with your partner—can strongly enhance your sexual desire.

This is important because it puts *you* in the driver's seat when it comes to your sexual desire. Even if you don't feel desire at the beginning of a sexual encounter with your mate, if the two of you start kissing and caressing, these research findings indicate that your desire will start to heat up, and you will end up thoroughly enjoying the lovemaking experience.

Sexual discrepancy also, unfortunately, can get entangled in the power struggle aspects of a relationship. When one partner's desire is significantly higher, or lower, than the other, it can lead to a variety of painful and distancing results as each partner fights and struggles for what they want and need. Read on for valuable tips and strategies to help if you and your partner are caught in the power struggle of differing levels of sexual desires:

♦ If you are the person with lower desire, act on *any* small urges or flickers of desire. People with low levels of desire don't tend to experience sexual desire as a raging inferno or an intense, almost overpowering craving. Rather, they experience sexual desire as a more subtle low simmer or smoldering ember. Such individuals may want to act on this mild glimmer of desire, knowing that it is likely not going increase any higher on its own. This is one way that low-desire partners can go the extra mile for the sake of their relationship.

♦ Sex and relationship experts remind us that adults who have made the decision to enter into intimate, committed relationships need to assume personal responsibility for their sexual desire, including boosting it, if need be. It's simply a part of being a mature person in a love relationship, a key component of the commitment that people make to their partners in any monogamous relationship or marriage.

♦ An effective way of assuming personal responsibility for enhancing your sexual desire is to explore your sensual nature to figure out exactly what turns you on. Even people with low desire have sexual triggers that put them in the mood for making love. For instance, some people feel turned on remembering a rewarding past sexual encounter with their partner. Others are able to boost their sexual desire by reading a sexy story (also known as erotica or romantica.) Or maybe burning scented candles is something you have long associated with romance and pleasurable sex. If this is the case, be sure to keep scented candles on hand at all times, and burn them as often as possible!

- If reading sexy material is your thing, read every sex book you can get your hands on ranging from how-to guides to books about the Kama Sutra to sexy works of literature. Learn about human anatomy and the different techniques people use to feel amorous and sexually aroused. The more you bring to the bedroom, in terms of your level of sexual knowledge, the better your chances are of boosting your sexual desire and enjoying sex. Once you've read all these materials and thoroughly educated yourself about what turns other people on, don't be shy about exploring what turns *you* on and encouraging your partner to do the same.

- Show your desire who is boss! As part of your sexual exploration process, work on identifying specific thoughts and fantasies that make you feel tingly and aroused. Don't fret that you might be lacking in the imagination department if you find that you enjoy revisiting certain tried and true thoughts and fantasies over and over again. On the contrary, if there are certain sexy scenarios you like to think about again and again before and during sex with your partner, think of them as your loyal friends and be sure to call upon them whenever you want to get yourself ready for love-making.

- Some people find keeping a locked, secret sex journal of all of their most risqué sexual thoughts, fantasies and desires can significantly enhance their level of sexual desire in a variety of ways. For starters, many people find it sexually stimulating to write down their sexual thoughts. Secondly, many people find it exciting to read these thoughts at a later time. And thirdly, some people find it thrilling to read some of their sexual thoughts out loud to their partner. Of course, there may be parts that they choose to keep to themselves, thus the importance of keeping it locked!

- If there is a specific occasion when your partner really wants sex, but you are really not in the mood, and can't get yourself in the mood, rather than turning your partner down flat consider saying something like: "I'm sorry, honey. I'm just way, way too tired tonight, so how about we take a rain check and make love tomorrow night instead?" And then be sure to keep your promise. In this way, the partner with a higher level of desire does not feel rejected, and you can both experience the sexy anticipation of knowing that you will be making love the following night.

◆ Making love on a regular basis helps both men and women produce more testosterone, which is the primary hormone of sexual desire. More specifically, regular sexual stimulation and sexual activity causes the body to increase its production of oxytocin, which in turn increases the production of endorphins (also known as the feel-good hormones) as well as the production of testosterone. And since we know testosterone is the hormone that is most responsible for causing both men and women to feel sexual desire, it naturally follows that the more testosterone your body produces, the more you will want sex. So yes indeed, one of the best ways—both physiologically and psychologically speaking—to increase your level of sexual desire is for you and your partner to have sex more frequently.

◆ If you have lower sexual desire than your partner, but you have been working on increasing your level of desire, give yourself a big pat on the back. Commend yourself for your efforts. Change is not easy, but by taking the time to figure out how to boost your sexual desire, you and your partner will reap many rewards.

◆ If you are the partner with the higher level of sexual desire, don't pressure your partner too much. It's not sexy, and it certainly won't make your partner want you more. After all, no one wants to feel they have been nagged or guilt-tripped into having sex. This kind of behavior can create an ugly interpersonal dynamic and it does absolutely nothing to foster feelings of closeness or emotional intimacy. Remember, most women need to feel a strong emotional connection with their partners to experience feelings of sexual desire.

◆ One more tip for partners with greater sexual desire: if it's evident your partner has been making a huge effort to change, please be sure to express your appreciation and encouragement frequently and enthusiastically. Everyone needs to feel encouraged and appreciated by their partners at all times, but perhaps especially when they are trying their hardest to enhance their level of sexual desire.

And a final bit of advice for everyone, regardless of your current level of sexual desire: Having an exciting, mutually rewarding sex life is a two-way street, particularly in a relationship with a sexual desire gap. Both partners need to be willing to give of themselves, to compromise, and to make any necessary changes in their attitudes and behaviors. Most of all, enhancing sexual desire in any intimate relationship (not only in relationships with desire gaps), requires both partners to refuse to play the blame game, and to engage in an ongoing, open, honest dialogue about their shifting sexual needs and desires. In other words, it requires a "we're in this together" attitude.

Women and Hormones

Hormones shape your sex drive from puberty onward. Your hormone levels are constantly fluctuating throughout the different phases of your menstrual cycle, pregnancy, childbirth, lactation, perimenopause, and menopause. Any of these fluctuations can cause your sexual desire to spike or plunge, so be aware of the role your hormones play in causing your sex drive to increase or decrease at different points in your life; remember that you can talk with your doctor about it.

Giving Birth and Breastfeeding

Some (though certainly not all) women experience temporary damage to their pelvic nerves and muscles from childbirth. This can temporarily lower their sensitivity to sexual stimulation.

Also, lactation (i.e., breastfeeding) can simultaneously cause production of a hormone called prolactin (which dampens desire) to increase, and production of estrogen (which enhances desire) to decrease.

In addition, approximately 10 percent of pregnancies result in postpartum depression, which can significantly curb sexual desire. Women can experience postpartum depression anywhere from a few days to few months after giving birth.

Fortunately, chances are that if you lose some sexual sensitivity following childbirth, you will likely regain it soon. Also, you won't be breastfeeding forever, so you can rest assured that the desire-dampening hormonal changes associated with lactation are temporary.

There are several treatment options for all forms of depression, including postpartum depression, so consult your physician if you believe you are experiencing any degree of postpartum depression. We will discuss more about depression later in this appendix.

The Pill

Many women take "the Pill" to prevent pregnancy. However, it can also impede your sex drive because it causes your ovaries to "sleep" for 3 out of 4 weeks each month. Your ovaries not only produce eggs, but they also generate the hormones that stimulate your sex drive. So for women on the Pill, their ovaries are not generating these sex hormones as they normally would. In addition, the Pill signals your system (specifically your liver), to manufacture more SHBG (sex hormone binding globulin). SHBG is a glycoprotein, or a "biomolicule" comprised of a protein and a carbohydrate, that attaches itself to sex hormones—especially testosterone, which is largely responsible for causing you to experience sexual desire—rendering these hormones ineffective by impeding their ability to circulate as "unbound" or "free" sex hormones.

If you are currently taking the Pill and are concerned that it may be negatively affecting your level of sexual desire, you may want to consult your physician about changing to another type of Pill or to a different form of birth control.

Infertility Issues

When a couple is having difficulty conceiving a baby, their relationship —and particularly their sex life—can suffer. Every time the woman is ovulating, the couple feels enormous pressure to have sex. And every month that she gets her period, the couple feels crestfallen. As you can well imagine, this pressure can dampen their sexual desire and take the joy and spontaneity out of their lovemaking.

If you are struggling with infertility, it can be helpful to join a support group with other couples who are experiencing similar problems. Also, talk with your doctor about treatments and solutions. Fortunately, we live in a time when there are several different treatment options available for infertile couples. These treatment options include medications such as clomiphene, artificial insemination, in-vitro fertilization (IVF), donor eggs and embryos, and gestational carriers (also known as surrogate mothers).

Some couples also report successfully treating infertility problems with acupuncture and Chinese medicines, though you will probably want to consult with your primary care physician before undergoing any kind of treatment.

Menopause

Some menopausal women experience diminished sexual desire as a result of the hormonal changes going on in their bodies. They may also experience a variety of other unpleasant symptoms, such as irritability, insomnia, mood swings, cloudy thinking, night sweats, hot flashes, and vaginal dryness.

Lifestyle Changes

Sometimes all of these menopausal symptoms—including diminished sex drive—can be effectively managed by making certain healthy lifestyle changes. These lifestyle changes include drinking more water, drinking less alcohol and caffeine, eating healthier foods, exercising more, and using stress-reduction techniques like yoga, meditation, stretching, deep breathing, and visualization.

Hormone Replacement Therapy

If lifestyle changes are not enough, hormonal treatments can be used to alleviate the unpleasant symptoms of menopause, including diminished sexual desire.

One mode of treatment that many doctors consider for menopausal women with severe symptoms is Hormone Replacement Therapy (HRT).

HRT is comprised of natural or synthetic female sex hormones (primarily estrogen). These hormones are introduced into the body in order to replace estrogen and the other hormones that are produced in significantly less quantity during menopause. HRT may be prescribed in the form of patches, gels, or tablets.

However, HRT (or any other hormonal treatment) is *never* prescribed for the sole purpose of enhancing a patient's level of sexual desire. There are too many possible health risks involved. HRT must always be used with caution and under strict medical supervision, because recent studies indicate that while it is effective for alleviating the symptoms of menopause, it may also increase a woman's risk of developing heart disease, breast cancer, and stroke.

These risk factors have made HRT the subject of serious debate in the medical community. Remember, there are always health risks any time patients introduce doctor-prescribed hormones into their bodies.

If you are suffering from debilitating symptoms associated with menopause, consult with your physician about HRT before determining whether or not it is the best symptom-alleviating treatment option for you. Typically, as a safety precaution, this treatment option should be used for the shortest time needed to alleviate the symptoms, and at the lowest possible dosage.

Low-Dose Testosterone Treatment

While HRT can be effective for eliminating the negative symptoms of menopause, including diminished sexual desire, it is actually testosterone, and *not* estrogen, that is the hormone *most* strongly associated with feelings of sexual desire in both women and men.

This brings us to another treatment option for menopausal women with unpleasant symptoms: low-dose testosterone treatment. This form of treatment has been found to be particularly effective for enhancing sexual desire in younger women who have had their ovaries removed for medical reasons.

Low-dose testosterone treatment is usually administered via a skin patch, in gel form, or as a cream. While it is possible to ingest low-dose testosterone orally, most doctors prefer not to prescribe it this way, because it has been found to lower good cholesterol and raise bad cholesterol. Testosterone, the hormone of sexual desire, is known primarily as a male hormone, or androgen. Both men and women produce testosterone, albeit in vastly differing quantities. A woman produces the most testosterone she will ever produce at around the age of 20. This amount declines steadily over time. Many studies indicate that low-dose testosterone treatment, administered in conjunction with estrogen, can be extremely effective for menopausal and postmenopausal women who have experienced a precipitous drop in their sexual desire.

This form of treatment should always be closely monitored by a doctor, and once again for the safety of the patient, typically only be administered for a short period of time and at the lowest possible dosage. When testosterone is taken by female patients at too high of a dose, and/or without estrogen to balance it out, it can cause male-type physical traits, such as male pattern baldness, a deep voice, and/or a decrease in breast size.

Natural Treatments for Menopause

Natural treatment options are also available for menopausal women with unpleasant symptoms, including diminished sexual desire. For instance, certain herbs such as Muirapuama, particularly when taken in conjunction with another herb, ginkgo biloba, have shown promise for enhancing sexual desire. Similarly, some women feel they have benefited from increasing their dietary intake of soy and/or black cohosh, a plant-based alternative to hormone replacement therapy, known commercially as remifemin.

In addition, some women swear by certain botanical oils, such as Zestra, as an effective means of stimulating their sexual desire. Zestra is available over the counter and you can use it during intimate touching, massage, and foreplay with your partner to enhance your sexual desire and arousal.

When trying any natural remedies, however, always exercise caution and consult your doctor. And never exceed the recommended dosage. After all, even so-called natural cures such as herbs may cause unwanted side effects in some people. Also, the possible medical risks associated with taking such herbs and plant products are not yet fully known or understood by the medical community.

Medications

Certain medications you are on can cause your sex drive to decrease. For instance, medications to lower blood pressure can reduce sex drive. Antihistamines, which are taken to dry up runny noses can also decrease a woman's vaginal lubrication, which can in turn make sex significantly less enjoyable (and therefore not as desirable).

Other medications that can dampen sexual desire in both women and men are the SSRIs (or selective serotonin reuptake inhibitors) such as Prozac (generic name: fluoxetine) or Paxil (generic name: paroxetine).

If you are currently taking an SSRI for the treatment of depression, and you are concerned that it may be causing your sexual desire to plummet, you may want to ask your doctor about Wellbutrin (generic name: bupropion), a dopamine reuptake inhibitor. Wellbutrin has been found to elevate sexual desire in some individuals. Of course, any medication may have negative side effects, so be sure to talk to your doctor about them.

Depression

Depression can be triggered by a number of psychological and physical conditions, including work-related stress, terminal illness, or childbirth to name a few. In addition to making you feel sad and empty inside and altering your appetite, eating habits, and sleep patterns, depression can also dampen your sex drive. Indeed, a lack of sexual desire is considered one of the chief symptoms of depression.

Depression is very serious. If you are concerned that you may be depressed, it's very important you talk to your doctor or a therapist about it right away, to figure out suitable treatment options for you.

Although certain antidepressant medications, namely the SSRIs like Prozac, can reduce desire, it's dangerous to ignore any symptoms of depression.

Depression in Men

It's important for us to note here that clinical depression in men is often underrecognized and underdiagnosed, in part because there is a great deal of societal pressure for men who feel depressed to "just suck it up" and not ask for help.

If you think your partner, or any other male loved one, could be suffering from depression, we strongly recommend Terrence Real's highly informative books on the subject: *I Don't Want to Talk About It* and *How Can I Get Through to You?* Talk with your partner about how he is feeling and let him know it's okay to seek help.

Drugs and Alcohol

Many people believe using alcohol and drugs can make them less sexually inhibited. However, the excessive use of illicit drugs, tobacco, and/or alcohol can severely dampen your desire for sex, as well as your capacity to enjoy it, not to mention it impairs motor functioning. So, if you think you or your partner may have a problem with substance abuse, seek help from your doctor, a counselor or loved ones.

Health Problems

Certain medical conditions can affect a person's blood flow, nerve signals, and hormone levels, all of which play key roles in determining her level of sexual desire. These conditions include high blood pressure, high cholesterol, diabetes, and thyroid problems. They also include illnesses that compromise the autoimmune system, such as lupus.

Fortunately, your physician can prescribe medications to help with these health problems. And often, once these medical conditions have been successfully treated, your sexual desire will return.

Finding the Right Doctor

Because we have advised and emphasized the importance of seeking medical help and treatment for various causes and conditions of low sexual desire, it is equally important to emphasize the need for finding the right doctor for your condition and for you.

Some doctors minimize the importance of a low sex drive in their patients' lives and may brush aside complaints of diminished desire, as if it is a minor problem or side affect not be taken too seriously. But it is not a problem to be taken lightly or discounted! Low and no sexual desire can do significant harm to your relationship and your sense of self-esteem.

Understanding, empathetic doctors realize this and will address it and give it the necessary attention. So please search until you find a doctor who understands and is addressing with you the true importance of your sexual desire issues. On a similar note, if your partner is currently struggling with low or no sexual desire, but has been reluctant to see a doctor about it, you may want to encourage him or her to do so. Perhaps you could start by reminding your partner that there are now several excellent, highly effective treatment options available.

Pressure and Stress

We talked extensively in this book about stress and how it can throw a wet blanket on your sex life. When you feel overwhelmed by obligations and responsibilities, it can perceivably reduce your sexual desire and make it difficult for you to unwind, relax, and enjoy yourself sexually with your partner. In extreme cases, it can cause depression.

If pressure and stress in your life have gotten so extreme that you have lost your sense of sexual desire, remember, as we discussed in the book, what a fantastic stress reliever sex can be. It can be as simple as working with your partner to implement the techniques and strategies provided in this book. But if you find those are not working, your problem may be physical or something more than you can manage on your own and with your partner. If this is the case, seek help to find treatment options that can get you back on track and enjoying sex again.

Current Relationship Issues

Sometimes sexual problems—including a lack of sexual desire—are symptomatic of other issues that may be going on in the relationship. If the two of you have been bickering constantly, or not communicating well, or not connecting on an emotional level, these problems can put a huge damper on your sexual desire.

To reconnect sexually, you may need to reconnect emotionally first. Men and women are a little different in this regard. Men often feel emotionally close by having sex. When they aren't having sex regularly with their partners, they tend to feel emotionally distant. Women, on the other hand, usually don't feel like making love unless they feel emotionally close first.

Of course what all of this means is that the two of you may need to have some challenging but necessary conversations to get back to a place of safety, trust, honesty, openness, and sexual and emotional intimacy.

Past Relationships Issues

As we have observed, sometimes people are haunted by the ghosts of their past relationships. This is just another way of saying that your past relationship experiences can color and affect your perception of your present relationship.

Perhaps one of you dated someone who was unfaithful, or who did not consistently treat you with loving kindness, or who coerced you into having sex before you were ready. Your negative sexual and emotional experiences with that individual can sometimes sneak up on you at the most unexpected times to cause you problems in the here and now.

Even if your current relationship is a source of emotional strength and support, it's important for you to pay attention to your feelings when bad memories from past relationships pop up in your mind.

You may want to talk to your partner when these bad memories arise, to give you the chance to vent your anger and sadness about them. It also gives your partner the chance to validate your feelings, express his unconditional love and support for you, and assure you that he is not anything like "that other guy."

In addition, if any of your past negative sexual experiences are causing you to feel sexually inhibited in your current relationship, the two of you can work on resolving these problems *together* with gentle, consistent use of the three Ts of sexual teamwork: time, talk, and touch.

Sexual Trauma and PTSD

PTSD (Posttraumatic Stress Disorder) is a pathological anxiety that develops after a person experiences or witnesses a severely traumatic event. Such events include war, a natural disaster, a serious automobile accident, rape (or any other form of sexual assault), physical assault, the diagnosis of a life-threatening illness, or any other trauma that presents a threat to the life or safety of that individual or of another individual.

In the direct aftermath of the traumatic experience, the person feels fearful, helpless and horrified. After the passage of time, individuals with PTSD develop several or all of the following symptoms: numbness, avoidance, hyperarousal, intrusive thoughts and/or dreams about the event, and/or the sensation of continually reliving the traumatic experience. These individuals often find it difficult to function in their day-to-day lives, including their workplace and relationships.

If you think that you may be suffering from PTSD as a result of one or more traumatic past sexual experiences, we strongly advise you to seek counseling from a therapist who specializes in this area. After all, it will be difficult (if not impossible) for you to experience healthy sexual desire or to enjoy your sex life with your partner until you address your PTSD-related issues.

If you or your partner suffer from PTSD or are considering undergoing a psychological evaluation to determine as such, this is in no way a reflection of a lack of emotional strength. Certain traumatizing experiences (including rape or any kind of sexual assault) are so devastating and destructive that even emotionally resilient people can experience PTSD symptoms long after experiencing the traumatic events.

Please note not all individuals who undergo traumatic experiences end up developing PTSD. But even if you are not suffering from the symptoms of PTSD, if you have undergone one or more sexual traumas, consider going to therapy to work through your feelings about these traumas and learn ways to find greater happiness and fulfillment in your current sexual relationship.

Maybe your negative sexual experiences were not traumatizing, but might more accurately be described as unpleasant, boring or disappointing. Perhaps you suspect these negative (but non-traumatic) experiences from your past are sabotaging your sex drive in your current relationship. If so, consider adopting Dr. Maddi's useful advice we discussed at length in Chapter 6: assume a "Commitment-Control-Challenge" attitude as a part of your overall effort to boost your sex drive.

So, to reiterate, if you have ever been raped, sexually coerced, or sexually assaulted or traumatized in any way, it's important to seek counseling with a therapist who specializes in treating sexually traumatized individuals. Again, as we have said, a trained trauma therapist can determine if you are suffering from PTSD (posttraumatic stress disorder), provide you with appropriate treatment, and teach you effective coping skills, so that you can learn how to manage your emotional pain and move forward in your life.

A particularly helpful online resource for this is www.rainn.org. RAINN stands for the Rape, Abuse, and Incest National Network. This website offers a wealth of information, including many excellent articles and contact information for counseling centers and rape crisis hotlines located throughout the United States.

When Therapy Can Help

Some people who are struggling with a low sex drive (or no sex drive at all) find it helpful to seek therapy from a professional who specializes in sex-related issues. Therapy can be individual, couples, or a combination of the two.

Finding the right therapist for you can be challenging, but search until you find the best match. There are various ways to find a good therapist. Some people ask their general practitioner for a list of therapists who specialize in sexual issues, whereas others prefer to ask a trusted friend for a recommendation.

In this day and age, it can also be useful to conduct an online search. For instance, try plugging the words "couples therapists" or "sex therapists" and the name of your state into your favorite search engine. (Remember that sex therapists are specially trained to help their clients deal with all aspects of their sexuality, including their level of sexual desire, so if sexual desire is your main concern, you may want to seek out the professional guidance and support of a sex therapist.) In addition, your insurance company may provide you with a list on counselors that they have contracted with to provide their customers service.

You will likely find not only listings of individual therapists in private practice in your state, but you will also find networks of couples therapists and/or sex therapists, such as your particular state's Association for Marriage and Family Counselors. Contacting an established association might be a good way to start your search for the right therapist. You know ahead of time that all of the counselors in the network have been pre-approved and have licenses in good standing.

Understanding Problems for Men

Throughout this book, we focused a great deal on low sexual desire in women, mainly because women report low sexual desire in significantly greater numbers than men do. However, men also experience a wide range of sexual problems, including low (or no) sexual desire, so this next section is geared toward men and the women who love them.

Erectile Dysfunction

Perhaps the most commonly discussed sexual problem that men experience is erectile dysfunction. This term refers to a man's difficulties with getting and/or sustaining an erection before and during sex.

Some of the possible emotional causes of erectile dysfunction include stress, anxiety, relationship problems, and/or depression. Often it is necessary to treat these emotional problems with medication, therapy, or both.

Some medications specifically target erectile dysfunction. These include Viagra (generic name: sildenafil), Cialis (generic name: tadalafil), or Levitra (generic name: vardenafil). All of these medications have been clinically proven to help men overcome this upsetting problem.

Also, some medications can cause erectile dysfunction as a side effect in some men while helping the problem he is taking the medication for.

Some of the physical causes of erectile dysfunction include fatigue; the use of alcohol, drugs, and/or tobacco; brain and/or spinal-cord injury; certain prostate or bladder operations; radiation therapy to the testicles; Parkinson's disease; multiple sclerosis; stroke; liver and/or kidney failure; diabetes; high blood pressure; atherosclerosis (or hardening of the arteries); and/or hypogonadism, a medical condition that can lower one's testosterone levels. Be sure to check with your doctor and pharmacist about the side effects of any medications you or your partner is taking for any of these problems and what can be done if you have the erectile dysfunction side effect from them.

Men's Reduced Sexual Desire

Some men experience reduced sexual desire at some point in their lives, and for many of the same reasons as women. However, the number of men who report low sexual desire or no sexual desire is significantly lower than the number of women who report this same problem.

Some possible causes of low or no sexual desire in men are similar to those that cause erectile dysfunction. They include stress, depression, a low testosterone level, lack of sleep, excessive alcohol and/or drug use, certain diseases (such as diabetes, anemia and Parkinson's Disease), relationship troubles, certain prescription medications (such as SSRI antidepressants), and/or other health problems.

Men who undergo medical treatment for their underlying health problems often find that their sexual desire increases as well. Similarly, men who are experiencing lower sexual desire (or no sexual desire at all) as a result of relationship problems may find a solution in individual therapy, couples therapy, or a combination of the two.

Testosterone Therapy for Men

When a healthy man turns 40, his testosterone levels start to decline naturally, and at a gradual rate. Among other things, testosterone is responsible for a man's muscle mass, strength, bone mass, sperm production, potency, and sexual desire. While nearly all men experience this perfectly natural, gradual decline, their testosterone levels tend to stay within the normal range throughout their lifetimes.

However, approximately one in five men over the age of 60 undergoes a significant drop-off in testosterone production, a decline that can in turn cause his sexual desire to diminish dramatically as well.

Some men who experience this problem opt for testosterone therapy. However, this form of treatment for otherwise healthy male patients is not without controversy in the medical community, because not enough clinical tests have been performed to determine its long-term safety and effectiveness.

It's also important to note that researchers have found a clear link between male testosterone therapy and breast cancer in men. In particular, male patients with a family history of prostate cancer and/or breast cancer are urged to proceed with caution. Indeed, all healthy male patients who are considering undergoing a course of testosterone therapy for any reason—including the enhancement of their sexual desire—need to talk with their doctors and carefully weigh all of the pros and cons before beginning this form of treatment.

Keeping Sex Drive Issues in Perspective

Don't allow your sex-drive struggles to take over your whole life. Problems with sexual desire are certainly not enjoyable. But at the same time, sex-drive issues need not become the end of the world, either. Obsessing about diminished desire will not help you resolve the problem. It may even make it worse, because excessive worry is one of the factors that can lower your sexual desire.

Remembering Sexual Teamwork

As we have discussed, a couple's sex life is bound to ebb and flow over time. We are not static beings, after all, and nothing is ever permanent. For example, health factors may have affected your sexual desire. If you and/or your partner are currently experiencing significantly diminished (or nonexistent) sexual desire, remember that the solution lies in collaborating as a fully united sexual team. If the two of you work together on enhancing your mutual sexual desire and/or seeking treatments for medical or psychological problems related to your reduced sexual desire, you can regain the satisfying, exciting sexual relationship you both so richly deserve.

Further Reading

Other valuable resources for combating low or no sexual desire are Barry and Emily McCarthy's *Rekindling Sexual Desire*, Michele Weiner Davis's *The Sex-Starved Marriage*, Judith Reichman's *I'm Not in the Mood*, and Cristina Ferrare's *Okay, So I Don't Have a Headache*.

If the two of you are looking for some erotic—yet educational—ways to enhance your mutual sexual desire, try reading aloud from these sexy books: Eve Salinger's *The Complete Idiot's Guide to Pleasing Your Man* and *The Complete Idiot's Guide to Pleasing Your Woman*. You might enjoy reading together *Your Long Erotic Weekend*, by Lana Holstein and David Taylor.

Finally, if communication and intimacy problems have been ongoing issues in your relationship, try reading and discussing with each *The Seven Principles for Making Marriage Work*, by John Gottman and Nan Silver and/or *Mating in Captivity: Reconciling the Erotic and the Domestic*, by Esther Perel.

All of these titles are included in Appendix A as well.

Index

H

I

T